LUCKY LUCIANO:
MYSTERIOUS TALES OF A GANGLAND LEGEND

CHRISTIAN CIPOLLINI

13-digit ISBN 978-1939-5211-2-5
10-digit ISBN 1-9395211-2-2

CONTENTS

CHAPTER ONE

THE MAN BEHIND THE MYTH

GANGSTERS, HOODS, THUGS, racketeers, commonly nothing more than sheer denizens of normalcy, happily shunning the concept of law and order. Yet there is a broad love affair the public seems to hold with tales of their kind. Why are we, the purveyors of pop culture and controversy, so enamored by their stories, exploits, and history? Are we amazed and bewildered by the audacity of such criminal mischief? Do we secretly crave having seemingly endless power and wealth to wield? Are we just entertained, perhaps living a little vicariously through the legends of those almost-surreal lives? Maybe we just all like true tales of good versus evil, but sometimes the 'hero' we cling to isn't necessarily the protagonist of these stories. The anti heroes and antagonists are, sometimes, the most fascinating of characters – especially when the story is true. Then again, if it weren't for many of the undeterred and clever law enforcement entities throughout the history of gangland drama… there would be few stories, if any. The outlaws in these tales often do not easily volunteer, unless under extreme legal duress, the details we crave.

The authorities and media zealots (though often sensationalizing) carried to task the duties of filling our knowledge hungry minds with the salacious, seedy, surreal and scathing details of organized criminals and the vice-ridden manipulates. Murder, treachery, smuggling, thievery... just a few examples.

The legends of such criminal masterminds, names like John Dillinger, "Machine Gun" Kelly, Al Capone, Frank "Black Caesar" Matthews, Benjamin "Bugsy" Siegel among them, are entertaining, educational, and even scandalously fun to read about. However, since the dawn of storytelling, solid facts are not always there. Honestly, unless you were literally *there* during some of the more infamous adventures these characters embarked on... well, you won't ever really be able to know the whole story. Those truths and facts are more often interred with the bones of the individuals that lived it. Where there are always opportunities for further research, theorizing and most importantly, debating and discussing the many mysteries of the American gangland underworld.

And now we embark on a journey that has certainly been taken by many other scholars, researchers and historians before. The legendary Charles "Lucky" Luciano, with all the pomp and circumstance, is a subject that takes on a life of its own. His tale has been dissected, discussed, and debated for nearly a century. His role in the underworld has been scrutinized, over amplified, canonized, vilified, demonized, and even celebrated. So who was Lucky Luciano? Some believe he was the catalyst that changed the structure of organized crime, on a national level – for the better. Others believe he was not quite as important as legend would suggest – at least within a few of the many stories that were held as fact for many years.

Trying not to reinvent the wheel or venture into the realm of pretentiousness, this book will present a series of stories, myths and rumors that whirled around Luciano's archetypal role in crime, history and culture. Some of these tidbits are iconic stories themselves; others are a little less known. All are filled with amazing, often bizarre circumstances. Hopefully, each tale will entertain, titillate and open the doors to further discussion and debate over the man some call "The Chairman of the Mob." His scars, the nickname, the hits, the misses, the rumors, the girlfriends, the crimes and crime stoppers – these are the mysteries of a gangland legend.

First, a brief timeline of some significant events that helped shape the life and crimes of Charles "Lucky" Luciano:

Salvatore Lucania
Aliases: Charles Lucania, Charlie Lucky, Charles Ross, and Charles "Lucky" Luciano

1897: Born in Lercara Friddi, Sicily.

1906: Luciano's father Antonio arrives in New York.

1907: His mother, Rosalia, takes rest of family to New York.

1914: Harrison Narcotics Tax Act. Regulates cocaine and opiates.

1916: Luciano's first major brush with the law. Narcotics violation.

He is member of Five Points Gang (Al Capone is also a member)

1919/1920: Volstead Act. Designed to further enforce the 18th Amendment – Prohibition.

1920's: Luciano begins associations with Frank Costello, The Bug & Meyer Mob, Arnold Rothstein, George Uffner, Frank Erickson, The Diamond Brothers Gang, Vincent "Jimmy Blue

Eyes" Alo and Joe "The Boss" Masseria.

1928: Arnold Rothstein is murdered.

1929: St. Valentine's Day Massacre in Chicago. Al Capone believed responsible.

Luciano is a member of alleged bootlegging coalition called *The Seven Group or the Big Seven.*

Atlantic City Conference is held by Nucky Johnson to deal with bootlegging wars.

Later that year, Luciano is found beaten, scarred and left for dead under mysterious circumstances.

Stock Market Crashes – The Great Depression begins.

1931: Luciano orchestrates the murders of two major Mafia leaders: Joe Masseria - ending the Castellammarese War - and Salvatore Maranzano.

1933: 18th Amendment repealed. End of Prohibition.

1935: Flees impending law enforcement scrutiny, to Hot Springs Arkansas, a gangster friendly location.

1936: Luciano extradited back to New York. Convicted and Sentenced for "Compulsory Prostitution." Begins serving 30 to 50 year prison sentence.

1941: United States enters World War II.

1942: Seized French Ocean Liner, *Normandie*, catches fire in New York Harbor while being converted to a troopship. Paranoia and suspicions lead to sabotage theories.

Office of Naval Intelligence decides to make underworld allies, in hopes of protecting the mob-controlled docks from Nazi sabotage.

1943: Through intermediaries Meyer Lansky, Frank Costello, attorney Moses Polakoff and others, Luciano appears to have offered assistance to the war effort at home and abroad.

1946: Governor Thomas E. Dewey commutes the sentence (in

return for Luciano's presumed Allied war effort), under stipulation Luciano exiled to Italy and not permitted to ever return to United States.

From Italy, Luciano then visits Cuba, attends large meeting of top mobsters in Havana. Legends of the meeting reveal Benjamin Siegel's death sentence is issued because of missing money and poor results of the Flamingo Hotel project in Las Vegas.

1947: United States threatens to cut off medical narcotics supply to Cuba until Luciano is deported back to Italy. Cuban authorities comply and deport Luciano.

In June, Benjamin "Bugsy" Siegel is assassinated in the Beverly Hills home of girlfriend Virginia Hill.

1948: Luciano meets Igea Lissoni. She is twenty years his junior, but quite possibly the one true love of his life.

1950: Kefauver Hearing begin, investigation of Interstate Crime. Many mob-affiliated individuals are called before the committee over a two-year period, including Meyer Lansky, Frank Costello and Virginia Hill.

1957: Apalachin Meeting. Mafia meeting in Apalachin New York raided by police, allegedly on tip from Meyer Lansky. Legend states Lansky, Costello and even exiled Luciano wanted to put a halt to Vito Genovese power trip.

1958: Igea Lissoni loses her battle with breast cancer.

1959: Cuban Revolution ends with Fidel Castro and his rebels taking power.

This is effectively the end of mob rule in Cuba.

Old pal of Luciano, George Uffner, dies in plane crash.

1962: Luciano dies of a heart failure, at a Naples airport, while meeting with American movie producer Martin Gosch, who is planning a book with co-author Richard Hammer.

A grand funeral is held in Italy.

Luciano's remains are brought back to New York, buried in Queens.

1963: McClellan Hearings. Organized Crime investigation, made famous for mobster Joseph Valachi's tell-all testimony on the mob's long history.

1968: Gambler pal of Luciano, Frank Erickson, dies at age 72.

1973: Martin Gosch dies. His wife, allegedly, destroys or throws out all of Gosch's hand written notes taken in meetings with Luciano.

"Prime Minister of the Underworld," Frank Costello dies from throat cancer.

1975: The controversial book *The Last Testament of Lucky Luciano* is released. To this day... the book has been scrutinized as, at least partially, manufactured or fictionalized by co-author Richard Hammer. Most historians do not use the book as a legitimate source of information, though Hammer maintains the bulk of the text is from Luciano's own mouth.

1983: The last of Luciano's closest pals, Meyer Lansky, dies at age 80 in Miami.

CHAPTER TWO

ORIGINAL GANGSTERS

Gangster: noun: *a member of an organized group of violent criminals.*

Related Terms: *hood, racketeer, mobster, hooligan, hoodlum, thug, Mafioso, ruffian, crook, tough.*

HE WAS NOT a lone wolf outlaw, nor any sort of Robin Hood. Charles "Lucky" Luciano certainly had a band of murderous men with him, and without those numerous alliances and followers, he would not have been so powerful in his pinnacle moments. It is, therefore, virtually impossible to tell the tales of Charles "Lucky" Luciano without mentioning a laundry list of criminal compatriots. Each of his mob allies, enemies and loose associates had their very own stories (some as elusive and amazing as Luciano's). In this particular expose of Lucky's life and surrounding mysteries, there is a specific group of gangsters who can, arguably, be called the *Originals*. Some of the names and backgrounds are familiar territory for those long fascinated with the history of organized crime. Other individuals, even for the aficionado, may be of a limited or vague recognition. What all of these particular *O.G's* had in common was a man named Rothstein.

During the heyday of Arnold Rothstein's stranglehold on underworld finance and gambling rackets, men like Luciano, Frank

Costello, Meyer Lansky, Benjamin "Bugsy" Siegel, Jack "Legs" Diamond, Thomas "Fatty" Walsh, Frank Erickson, Vincent "Jimmy Blue Eyes" Alo and George Uffner co-mingled quite a bit. They all had dealings with Rothstein; many had furthered their criminal education thanks to his tutelage. To be clear, Arnold Rothstein was not a "mob boss" per se, but rather a man with the mind and money to "back" illicit investments. All of these gangsters took part, some large and some small, in Rothstein's exploits.

Each of these mobsters was 'associated' with certain other gangs or dabbled in various criminal enterprises outside the Rothstein camp, and respectively had their own individual specialties. Luciano, for example, rose from the infamous Five Points Gang into 'officially' working for Joe "The Boss" Masseria, but carried on in thievery with the Diamond Gang. Legs Diamond was the head of his own little gang, obviously, yet was involved with Rothstein in bootlegging. Lansky and Siegel were the heads of the Bug and Meyer Mob, running a protection racket, and developed a close friendship with Luciano. Walsh served, concurrently, as Rothstein's bodyguard and a Diamond Boys thug. Frank Erickson was mastermind of gambling, a master bookie in the Rothstein realm. George Uffner was the main point of narcotics traffic, of which Rothstein had interests. Frank Costello, an old pal of Uffner, could be compared to a social media guru of today's world. He was diplomatic, and always able to "pay" for favors the mob was in need of.

George Uffner, Frank Erickson, Vincent Alo are names that don't quite resonate in the collective pop culture mind like some of the others. Nevertheless, they were all key figures in the development of many underworld fortunes. Uffner and Erickson were the least recognizable gangsters of the lot, simply by keeping much lower key than even Meyer Lansky (who supposedly often reminded Lucky to avoid being flashy and noticeable) and certainly nothing like the flamboyant, media-hounded "Legs" Diamond.

The multi-ethnic cooperation under Rothstein was likely a contributing factor in Luciano's rise in underworld hierarchy. Having grown up in a largely Jewish part of town, plus working with non-Italians on a regular basis in the 1920's, Luciano's view of how business should operate was in great contrast to the Mafia system. Furthermore, he was probably becoming aware of how limited the opportunities are when an organization – like his boss Masseria's – shuns doing business with other ethnic groups. Rothstein's stable of gangsters were multi-cultural opportunists, into just about every racket under the sun; booze, dice, dope, bribery, extortion included.

While all the original gangsters played their parts in Rothstein's world, they each ventured further into their own domains as the years passed. Then, in 1928, something went terribly wrong; actually it may have been a series of events that culminated in the headline making murder of Rothstein.

On November 4th, Rothstein was shot at the Park Central Hotel in Manhattan. He succumbed to the wounds two days later, without identifying his killer. Of all the gangland lore, Rothstein's murder may be one of the greatest unknowns. Most of what police found, in terms of speculation - Rothstein had not paid up on a gambling debt of over $300,000. Investigators pulled in witnesses and suspects from virtually all over the country, trying to sort out what happened. Fingers were pointed directly at a man named George McManus (he was eventually acquitted). In late November though, police grabbed three men for questioning; Lucania, Uffner and Walsh. All three denied having anything to do with Rothstein's murder. Walsh, whom authorities knew worked as a bodyguard for Rothstein, claimed he was employed for just a few months in that capacity and that Rothstein was killed over a card game. It was discovered, however, that Walsh left the Rothstein job almost immediately following a large narcotics seizure that was traced to Rothstein. The connection was unclear, and certainly suspicious.

The three men were soon released, but there still remains conjecture or theories that Rothstein's murder may not have just been about owing money from card games. As the investigation continued, files were found containing information that led authorities to link drugs, leases to oilfields, and other investments to Rothstein. And, on the 19th of November, just a day after Uffner, Luciano and Walsh were released on bail, another Rothstein associate, Dr. Charles Brancati, disappeared... permanently.

Brancati was suspected to be in cahoots with Rothstein in the finance of narcotics and counterfeiting. His body was never found, but officials eventually declared him dead in 1932. Another acquaintance of Rothstein, Joseph Klein, was apprehended in December, on a train with a trunk full of narcotics – estimated at over $2,000,000 worth - linked directly to Rothstein as the backer.

In relation to the narcotics financing and what happened to some of Rothstein's other investments isn't entirely a mystery, according to one of George Uffner's relatives. A family source, who wished to remain anonymous, says some of the Uffner lineage believes George had *something* to do with Rothstein's death, or at the very least – what happened after the murder.

"I'm confident that they (original gangsters) played a major role in his death," claims the family source. "At one point they were all buddies, and something went wrong. I don't know if it was a debt, oil leases, or missing cash but, something went terribly south with Mr. Rothstein being the shyster as far as the OGs (original gangsters) were concerned."

The Family Source also says Uffner's descendants had long heard the stories of the Rothstein relationship between Uffner and Luciano, particularly with regard to the narcotics issue. "George Uffner travelled to the orient, and Middle East to secure large purchases of heroin with Arnold Rothstein's money. They used to smuggle the drugs in through the antique store in Manhattan called *La Vitrine.*"

Uffner's future wife – showgirl Evelyn Carmel - owned the store, says the Family Source. "Evelyn couldn't avoid the gangster scene after Arnold Rothstein opened up his famous gambling club right smack dab in the middle of the original Broadway. I'm very sure this is where she first met George "the money man" Uffner. This operation (the narcotics via antique store) lasted for years, and the Feds never figured out the antique shop in Manhattan that imported heroin by the pounds for so many years."

The Roaring Twenties are often thought of in terms of how the wealthy engaged in vice and debauchery. Alcohol was prohibited, gambling was illegal, but the economy was good and the public wanted their fun. But it's important to put into perspective why narcotics, particularly heroin, were such a big deal for Rothstein, Luciano, and Uffner. Money, just like from the sale of prohibited alcohol, was in abundance from heroin sales. Before the Harrison Act of 1914, heroin was legally available in the United States. The drug could be purchased in various forms, right out of a mail order catalog! And similar to the issue with banning alcohol, people still wanted it. Moreover, there were hundreds of thousands of people estimated to have been already addicted to the ultra powerful opiate by the time it was regulated by the act.

Not everyone could get a doctor's excuse for it. Again, just like alcohol, gangsters swooped right in to supply the demand.

After Rothstein's death, some of the documents from his office led investigators to unravel the narcotics smuggling in more detail. Other documents, however, disappeared before authorities could get them. The Uffner Family Source says some of these materials were leases, held as collateral from oilmen gamblers in debt. "Frank Erickson, George Uffner, Lucky Luciano, and Arnold Rothstein were all the recipients."

The source also presents a scathing allegation as to why Uffner eventually distanced himself from Luciano. "Lucky Luciano at one point became addicted to the prostitutes, and drugs. This is where his association with George began to cool."

Another twist in the connection to Rothstein unfolded a year later. "Fatty" Walsh met his maker under suspicious circumstances on September 7th, 1929. He was involved in a card game with three other men in the Miami Biltmore Hotel. A situation erupted into gunfire; bullets struck Arthur Clark (alleged to have been a former member of the Diamond Gang and Walsh's personal bodyguard) and "Fatty" Walsh. Clark's wounds were not life threatening, but Walsh was not so fortunate. There were witnesses, suspects and lots of theorizing that ranged from gambling debts to Cuban liquor quarrels as the motive. His death remained and some say his ghost has remained to haunt the hotel.

As for the other *Original Gangsters'* fates, well, Luciano and close pals Lansky, Costello and Siegel went on to re-organized organized crime in such a manner the nation had never seen. Jack "Legs" Diamond tried to secure a narcotics source in Europe during 1930 (Luciano was with him on the first leg of the trip), but the venture was a failure. Diamond was killed in December 1931.

George Uffner was caught and sentenced to prison for check forgery and grand larceny in 1933 (served a few years, then married Evelyn Carmel). And as for Vincent "Jimmy Blue Eyes" Alo, he kept a low profile, working in the background along with Lansky for many years in gambling operations. He died in 2001. Mayor La Guardia hunted down Frank Erickson, who managed to stay under the radar for quite some time. In 1939, they tried to nail him on vagrancy, but Erickson had an armored car show up filled with cash to disprove he fit the definition of *vagrant*. Erickson never served much jail time (once in Rikers) and was said have given much of his profits to charity.

CHAPTER THREE

NUMBERS OF THE BEAST

"Catering to the Beast in Man Made King of Lucky"
1962 headline from The Miami News

THROUGHOUT CHARLES LUCIANO'S rise from small time hood to world-renowned kingpin, the press, historians, and some law enforcement often recognized him as a key player in two specific groups, both distinguished by numerals: *The Seven Group* and *The Big Six*, as they came to be identified. The earlier association, *The Seven Group*, was a coalition of mobsters during prohibition determined to draw lines, set up rules and ultimately reduce bloodshed and law crackdowns on bootlegging operations. The prohibition era system, if in fact the group existed as such and created the plan, would have been the predecessor to the *National Crime Syndicate* or *Commission* established following Luciano's removal of Masseria and Maranzano in 1931.

Much of the information on this group and its membership was based on probability and logic. The big names in bootlegging, from New York to Detroit, were recognizable at the time, therefore it is reasonable to accept the 'big name player's' as members.

The pivotal moment, that tied such speculation all together, was a product of basic cause and effect: *The St. Valentine's Day Massacre* of 1929 and the heat it brought on all bootleggers. Because of the bloodshed and bad press of Al Capone's murderous rampage on Chicago bootlegging rival, George "Bugs" Moran, gangsters up and down the Eastern Seaboard and into the Midwest needed to convene, settle the problems once and for all, diplomatically. The man who would host such a monumental event? Enoch "Nucky" Johnson – the controversial political top dog in Atlantic City. None of what this theory suggests, considering the time period and names involved, would be out of the realm of possibility.

In light of that possibility, and some photographic evidence, there isn't much mystery to the basic foundation of the story. Nucky did indeed host some sort of meeting, in May of 1929, with Al Capone very present on the boardwalk for all the press and public to see (there is a famous photograph of Nucky and Al depicting this, though some challenge the authenticity). However, the *other* guests – the *Seven Group* – are subject to discussion. In fact, it is not concretely known who really were the members or if the presumed members were even present in Atlantic City during the legendary crime conference. Underworld meetings not held with fancy invitations and registered guest lists.

The Seven Group was comprised, originally, of seven factions representing several geographical and gang splinter groups, according to most historical references (one legend is that Luciano felt seven was a good name, a lucky number, and the group grew quickly beyond the number seven but kept the name). Many sources credit Luciano with designing the alliance, but there is no proof to support that. Again, the specific individuals representing each area or division are where gangland rumors take over. There has always been a core list of people – common to most sources – assumed to be members: Lucky Luciano, Meyer Lansky (was said to have been married in Atlantic City, during the week of the meeting), Frank Costello, Abner "Longy" Zwillman, Joe Adonis, Moe Dalitz, Benjamin "Bugsy" Siegel, Charles "King" Solomon, Nig Rosen, John Torrio and of course Alphonse "Scarface" Capone (who joined during the supposed convention meeting).

Other variations of the membership list include gambling guru Frank Erikson, the beer baron Arthur "Dutch Schultz" Flegenheimer, Jake "Greasy Thumb" Guzik and Waxey Gordon. Some lists even included Owney " The Killer" Madden - Irish bootlegger who co-owned the iconic Cotton Club.

Though some writings point to an Irish presence, albeit a limited one, most source materials seem to concur that Jewish and Italian gangsters were very much looking to squeeze the once-dominant Irish faction completely out (many Irish gangsters had assimilated into legitimate society by then anyway). If true, the lack of Irish representatives in Atlantic City would make sense. Similarly, the presence of Waxey Gordon is unlikely – as Meyer Lansky had allegedly become his enemy by the time of the convention. Also, and assuming any of these crime stars were there at all, notably not present were Joe "The Boss" Masseria and his mortal enemy Salvatore Maranzano. Again, men such as them – the Moustache Pete's – were not believers in the multi-ethnic unification. It is also possible many of the Luciano's allies, both Italian and Jewish, were already considering how 'eliminate' the old faction, so of course the Masserias and Maranzanos of the underworld would not have been invited or would have declined the invitation.

Marc Mappen, author of *"Prohibition Gangsters: The Rise and Fall of a Bad Generation"*, suggested in a May 23, 2013 interview with *Rutgers Today* that the Atlantic City Conference may have involved far fewer people than ever historically accepted as being present. Mappen told the publication, "The convention supposedly involved dozens of mobsters from around the nation and set up a national crime syndicate. It now looks more likely that the Atlantic City meeting had only a few attendees, and they focused on cooling off the gang wars in Chicago."

Because the only known photographic evidence depicts Capone and Nucky – but no other well known gangsters - there is reason to be skeptical over how such a large consortium of high level mobsters would have been in town for days, yet not be seen or photographed too. Essentially, the meeting was most likely designed to ease the tension of bootlegging warfare and Capone did volunteer to 'get arrested' in Philadelphia (on a minor charge) to take the heat off the whole Valentine's Day situation. If other gangsters, besides the Chicago faction, were present, there is no solid way to prove it. Furthermore, gangland violence didn't just cease to exist after the convention. A newspaper report in June of 1929 covered a tale of mistaken identity and torture of a dentist – who was falsely targeted by hoods on the hunt for gangster Joe Aiello. The man these assailants thought they had kidnapped, Joe Aiello, was mentioned as being present at the Convention to make mends with Capone. The article specifically discusses the Atlantic City Convention, and how a 'gangland truce was broken' afterward with the violent attack of this dentist.

Educated conjecture, and a basic understanding of how these mobsters worked out problems, makes the case for the Seven Group plausible though – as many of the purported members did unify and successfully undermine the national prohibition laws, plus a national crime syndicate did in fact develop several years later and that was also feat requiring much collusion, organization and agreement. In short, there probably was a *Seven Group*, which may have even met together in Nucky Johnson's stomping grounds, which in turn may have laid the groundwork for an even larger conglomerate of gang cooperation.

The only documented "insider" information regarding the stealthy *Seven Group* came in form of testimony during the tax fraud trial of Johnny Torrio in 1939. Labeled "The King of International Dope Smugglers," Jacob "Yasha" Katzenberg was convicted in 1938 for trafficking millions of dollars of heroin. He received a paltry ten-year sentence, but was called to testify because he had information on Torrio and details behind the birth and disintegration of the Seven Group.

Assistant U. S. Attorney Seymour Klein began questioning Katzenberg on the bootlegging days, specifically his and Torrio's roles.

"In the fall of 1932 was there an association formed?" Klein asked.

"Yes," replied Katzenberg. "It was known as the 'Big Seven.' I was a member of one of the groups."

Klein prodded for more details on the membership. Katzenberg obliged.

"The Newark organization, the Charlie Solomon group, the Atlantic City organization, the Boston organization, the Frank Reichman organization, the Philadelphia organization and the Providence organization," Katzenberg itemized. "There were a few more, but I've forgotten the names "

Klein wanted individual names, but convicted drug lord could only recall Joe Adonis, Charles "Lucky" Luciano, Frank Zagarino, and the man he had never personally met - known as

"Longy." Katzenberg did however remember many of the finer details, such as specifics regarding the money, payoffs and even what happened after the group disbanded.

He testified the group held offices in two locations: The hotels Belvedere and Belleclaire. The former was for 'executives' and the latter for 'retail.' Katzenberg also said his initial buy-in amount was $50,000, which he got back out when the group came to an end in 1933. At that time, changes were taking place with the Volstead Act and mobsters knew the end of prohibition was coming, so Katzenberg said that was when he entered the narcotics trade.

If "Yasha" Katzenberg's account of the Seven Group was true... most of information written on the subject would be incorrect, or at the very least – up for heated debate. Names like Zagarino and Reich are not commonly found in most resources that detail the enigmatic group. Additionally, it was generally accepted that the Seven Group was born sometime in the 1920's. Katzenberg's testimony, if accurate, told of the inception year being 1932 – almost the end of prohibition – which would imply the so-called National Syndicate and Commission would have already been formed or close to it. In any case, the one constant element that can be agreed upon, threaded through every version – the presence of Charles "Lucky" Luciano.

Another incarnation of catchy descriptors for the top mob rulers was *The Big Six*. Unlike the Seven Group, though, the gangsters themselves probably did not create this elite club. This was more of an easy way to label the movers and shakers of the next era. The media loved catch phrases and law enforcement liked to categorize criminal types. Interestingly, some sources refer to the original bootlegging union as the Big Six, but most often the term applies to post-prohibition. In both cases, the similarity in mysterious circumstance again goes back to membership lists. It was a matter of *who* was a member, according to *whom*. Like the mystery of the Seven Group's affiliates, the Big Six apparently had interchangeable names, depending on what source was providing the list. Granted, power struggles cause changes in top tier bad guys, so it is understandable such a list would be more fluid, or subject to frequent reevaluation than the iconic Seven Group – particularly in the eyes of law enforcement.

Following the October 1935 murder of Dutch Schultz, newspapers and law enforcement entities began using the moniker "Big Six" - at first in relation to John Torrio and Lucky Luciano's role in the assassination plot. Shortly after the 'hit' on Schultz and his men, Torrio and Luciano went to Florida. Authorities wanted to question both men, but were unable to force them back to New York. The semi-retired mentor of Al Capone, Torrio, had never fully left the underworld; he merely moved back to New York from Chicago and was active in what had become Luciano's domain. Media reports began regarding him as "in league" with the Big Six; Luciano of course was fully a member.

"The sextet was named as Charles (Lucky) Luciano, Jacob (Gurrah) Shapiro, Louis (Lefty) Buckhouse, Charles (Buck) Siegel, Meyer Lansky and Abe (Longey) Zwillman," stated a *Rochester Journal* article titled "Seek Capone Aid in Killing of Schultz."

The name-dropping within the syndicated article was a bit incorrect. Charles "Buck" Siegel was actually referring to Benjamin "Bugsy" Siegel and Louis "Lefty" Buckhouse was better known as Louis "Lepke" Buchalter. At the time of Schultz's death, this cast of characters was certainly among the top tier vice lords. Torrio, as referenced in other news and police reports, was never implicated as being a Big Six member, but still viewed as a counselor to the group. His name remained linked to the Big Six, but who the core individuals were, well, that just seemed to change like the weather.

On October 28th, 1935 – the Associated Press reported Torrio's rumored hatred of Dutch Schultz (for a bonding company deal gone bad), and that's why he was considered a key figure in the murder plot. Additionally, the article specifically noted that Torrio was "a partner of Ciro Terranova, Augie Pisano and Charles (Lucky) Luciano in the 'Big Six' policy syndicate."

By 1951, former mayor William O' Dwyer had his own idea of the underworld upper ranks. O'Dwyer was the District Attorney who, along with Burton Turkus, brought down the infamous enforcement arm (dubbed "Murder Incorporated" by the press) of the National Crime Syndicate during the early 1940's. When O'Dwyer sounded off for the Senate hearing, he listed five of the alleged *Big Six* as Luciano, Joe Adonis, Meyer Lansky, Willie Moretti and Benjamin "Bugsy" Siegel. Still, all those years gone by and one important name seemed to be absent from almost every incarnation of the Big Six membership lists, the "Prime Minister of the Underworld" – Frank Costello. Even odder – Bugsy had been dead for four years, yet still considered in the ranks.

During the 1951 hearings, Senate Crime Committee Chief Counsel, Rudolph Alley, finally asked O'Dwyer, "What about (Frank) Costello?" His reply to the query was vague, saying only that Costello's name was not among those he discovered during his investigation of *Murder Inc.* And to that end, he also did not provide an alternate sixth individual to his Big Six list. Like the Seven Group, Luciano's always seems to be the only constant.

CHAPTER FOUR

A SCAR IS BORN

WHILE CRUISING A relatively quiet and sparsely populated section of Hylan Boulevard on Staten Island in the very late hours of October 16th 1929, on-duty patrolman Henry A. Blanke was probably not expecting much action. The temperature was unusually warm for the autumn season; the top down on his older model Ford patrol car. Blanke approached an area of the road situated close to Huguenot Beach, approximately five miles from the precinct. It was there he would inadvertently play a key role in one of, if not *the* most, sensational and misreported underworld mysteries of all time.

The car headlights illuminated a highly unusual, horrific image coming into sight. There on the side of the road, stumbling in the sand, a disheveled and bloody figure was trying to gain some footing. Blanke immediately pulled the car over, parking right next to the visibly injured individual.

What the young beat cop could clearly see— this man looked as though he had been in a very serious vehicular accident. Blood dripped from his face and neck, eyes swollen nearly shut. He appeared to have wounds on his back as well. That injury was evidently quite bad, as Blanke could see blood soaked straight through dark overcoat the man was wearing. There were, however, no vehicles anywhere in the immediate vicinity, no debris on the road, and no obvious signs of any accident whatsoever.

The odd situation morphed into further mystery as the victim shakily made his way to Blanke's patrol car, tightly pressing a bloodied handkerchief to his face. He leaned in toward the cop and said; "Get me to a taxi and let get me out of here and I'll give you fifty bucks." Of course the officer had no intention of obliging the extraordinarily odd request. Instead, Blanke assisted the man into his car and drove back to Tottenville Station, where he planned to have an ambulance called. On the way, the officer realized the victim was also in a very confused state, not understanding where exactly he was. Informing him it was Staten Island simply put the man in a further state of disbelief.

Blanke got back to the precinct and continued a line of questioning before the medical staff loaded the still unidentified man into the ambulance. He offered neither his name nor much of an explanation of what happened to him, besides the comment, "I was taken for a ride." In gangland terms... anyone 'taken for a ride' generally does not come back; a one way ticket to the afterlife. Now the situation seemed more like an assault than accident.

The victim was transported to Richmond Memorial Hospital where Detective Gustave Schley arrived, ready to pick up where Blanke left off in questioning. Six hours after he was first discovered crawling his way along on that lonely stretch of sand and brush lined road– the truth was revealed. Salvatore Lucania was the man's formal name, as discovered in the morning hours of October 17. Patrolman Henry Blanke would have had no idea that he saved the life of a man who would eventually be called the 'Lord of New York Vice.' Blanke was just doing his job.

Although Lucania was basically an unfamiliar name and face to the Staten Island precinct personnel, it did not take long for Detective Schley to find out he was a very well known racketeer in Manhattan. His records showed at least five arrests, the one being in connection with Jack "Legs" Diamond and the two murders the Irish gangster was wanted for at the Hotsy Totsy Club. Although Lucky was working directly for Joe "The Boss" Masseria at the time, he was also chiefly associated with The Diamond Brothers Gang and a known acquaintance Arnold Rothstein's bodyguard Thomas "Fatty" Walsh. Lucania maintained, however, that he was merely a chauffer and had no idea why anyone would have roughed him up.

While Schley kept a close eye and ear on Lucania, a physician worked quickly to clean the wounds and patch him up. Lacerations were located on his back, neck, right-side cheek and throat area. There was residue across his mouth, left behind presumably from adhesive tape. His eyes were blackened; wrists and ankles bruised and cut from restraints of some kind. The doctor cleaned, stitched and bandaged the wounds as best he could. Schley was convinced Lucania, or Charlie Lucky as he was commonly known, had been kidnapped and beaten, but by *who* was another unsolved mystery. If it was an attempted robbery... the thieves weren't very efficient or Charlie lucked out in cleverly hiding his goods. He still had a shiny gold chain on, wristwatch, and then revealed over three-hundred dollars in cash he had neatly stashed inside a hidden pouch. After the medical work was complete, Lucania reached into his silk underpants and removed the money from its secret sewn in pocket. "Buy yourself a new shirt," he said to the physician, while handing over one hundred of the secretly stashed dollars. "Because you got all splattered up with my blood."

Lucania's version of the incident was vague at best. He told Schley three men, armed with pistols, forced him into a car, while he stood at Fiftieth Street and Sixth Avenue in Manhattan. The violence that followed, Lucania further explained, included beating and stabbing, before he claimed to pass out. He also told Schley that it was a situation he would "take care of himself."

Well, Charlie's request for the police to leave the whole incident alone, that was not going to be the case at all. Schley's research additionally provided information on Lucky's recent activities, leading him to believe there was much more to this story. Authorities were also very interested in speaking to him with regard to a Grand Larceny charge (stolen car, along with Legs Diamond's brother Eddie). So, before his swelling of his face and eyes could subside, Charlie Lucky was headed for a police lineup. Like most of his prior arrests, the charges against him were dropped shortly after his release from custody on October 29th. Lucky had survived a presumed 'death ride' and made averting jail time seem easy.

Lucky's version of events on the night of October 16th 1929 varied over the years, depending on with whom he spoke to. He told the original investigators that he had no idea who abducted and beat him, but it was three men. Sometimes he told the story as though two or four men manhandled him. He told others that it was cops behind it, seeking information on his criminal cohort Jack "Legs" Diamond (this is the version he remained most consistent in telling). He even went so far in detail, once, describing how he planned to get retribution on the police, but they paid him another surprise visit (claiming he narrowly escaped), forcing him to simply just renege the vengeance talk.

The media, and even many respected researchers, took a slew of inconsistencies and improbabilities for fact throughout the years as well. For quite some time the evildoers were considered to be fellow gangsters, sent on the order of Salvatore Maranzano. That particular tale is filled with horrific torture – Lucky strung up by his thumbs, beaten and having his throat slashed while dangling. Another version, arguably the most pejorative of them all, mentioned in the book *The Luciano Story* by Sid Feder and Joachim Joesten (and on the back of press circulated mug shot found in the author's collection), reported his trademark scars and droopy eye were a result of an angry father, or the more subversive - "beating by the father of the girl he tried to rape." This particular theory took on a life of its own, ranging from a simple date with the wrong girl to rape to pregnancy.

Which version is true? Only Lucky knew the answer in total certainty, but he left the world with much suspense and no clear-cut facts. However, more and more researchers and historians have come to consider the 'police brutality' theory as very plausible. Perhaps Lucky wasn't stabbed or slashed at all, and as Luciano himself suggested during one of his interviews. Lucky's injuries, he admitted, could have come from rings upon the fingers of those repeatedly beating on him. As he aged, Lucky never wavered much from the story that police roughed him up. Yet, there is another angle; an obscurity from 1962 that adds more fascinating and dynamic twists to the story, combining elements almost all of the previous legends into one peculiar interpretation.

But first… *there's the nickname*. Until quite recently, the story of Luciano's "Lucky" moniker has also widely been, and very mistakenly, attributed to his 'survival' on that fateful October night. Let's put one of these mysteries to rest right now – Salvatore Lucania was already known, by gangsters and cops alike, as *Charlie "Lucky"* before he was 'taken for a ride.' Not "Lucky" Charlie either. The name was always Charlie "Lucky."

By the time the story of his beating was reported (only one to two days after the incident in most papers), he was being referred to as though *Lucky* was the name by which everyone would have recognized him. It isn't difficult to understand how the name could be considered in relation to a survival tale. In fact, it's not at all hard to believe a story like that, especially when tied directly to the "gangland beating" version and being "taken for a ride." Still, if one mystery among the many that revolve around Charles "Lucky" Luciano can be solved – this is probably the one. Prior to the 1929 near death experience, he was known around town as Charlie "Lucky" Lucania. As for the nickname's backstory, well, some tales refer to Lucania's foray into crime, one that was based on early success (or luck) at illicit gambling. Another theory, which is even more probable, basically suggesting the various ethnic groups and subsequent language barriers in New York, of which Lucania was surrounded by and mingled among, may have had difficulty pronouncing his last name (loo-kah-nee-ah), and eventually a shorter, easier variation evolved. Some accounts, as told by his pal Frank Costello, even contradict themselves. Costello once said Lucky hated the name and nobody called it to him directly. Yet, another moment in time, Costello explained that Lucky created the name himself because people gravitate to the *lucky* ones.

In the 1950's, when the exiled to Italy, Luciano began granting numerous interviews to reporters visiting him. His response to columnist Leonard Lyon's very direct question, "Do you have any regrets?" further adds credence to *Lucky* being in existence well before the gangster ever took a ride. Luciano told Lyons, "Just one thing. These tattoos." Luciano was referring to a pair of tattoos he had acquired at age seventeen (he was thirty-two years old when the kidnapping and beating took place). Each forearm was inked; one was a nude woman, the other – the word "Lucky."

And about that droopy eye? This is yet another noteworthy aspect to address of Lucky's ordeal in 1929. To examine early photographs of Luciano, compared to post-*ride* photographs, reveals an obvious physical trait: Luciano had a slight 'sag' to his right eye before he was *taken for a ride*. The disfiguring after effect of assault most certainly added to the droop, but again, he already had a slightly sinister look long before the image was food for a frenzied media machine.

Now, back to the "ride" itself and the wildly ranging theories behind his assailants and their motives. Although Luciano often told interviewers similar versions of the same tale – cops did it because they wanted information on Legs Diamond – perhaps the least discussed, needle in a haystack alternative came from the very patrolman who rescued him.

Just weeks following Luciano's death in 1962, a reporter from the *Sarasota Herald-Tribune* paid a visit to the Englewood Florida home of Henry A. Blanke for an interview that turned out to be quite revealing. In the years following his fateful encounter with a bloodied Lucky Luciano, Blanke was promoted to detective and eventually retired from the force in 1955. He moved to Florida and raised a family only year thereafter. In all the decades that had passed – he never forgot how much of an impression on history that night in 1929 had made. In telling reporter Josephine Cortes the events of that night, many details remained consistent with most of all the other accounts– up until the part when Luciano goes to the hospital. The tale takes on an entirely different angle when Blanke recalled going back to the spot on Huguenot Beach a day after he found Lucky. There, he told the reporter, clues were found: cotton wad (presumably used in Luciano's mouth), adhesive tape, and the wire, he suspected, that had been used to bind Lucky's wrists and ankles. These however were not the most bizarre traces of evidence. Blanke said he noticed several sets of footprints in the sand… "Including the pointed toe and sharp heel made by a woman's shoes."

His further recollection included suspicions of a "Dark haired beauty" that investigators believed Lucky was actually waiting for in Manhattan before he was abducted. The unidentified woman, Blanke told the reporter, was the daughter of a New York detective. This account of the night goes hand in hand with, or could conceivably be the forbearer to the mysterious, "angry father," "rape" and "pregnancy" theories that apparently circulated at some point after the incident.

Still, the remaining features of Blanke's version take an opposing turn to the 'woman' theory, further making this entire legend more perplexing. The retired detective said within the weeks following Lucky's recovery – more than a few 'suspects' turned up dead. Cortes wrote of Blanke's recollection, "One was found in a river, encased in cement; another was found on a lonely road, his body riddled with bullets." Blanke evidently told her every individual on their list of possible perpetrators wound up dead. Those recollections are more in line with the now largely unaccepted story of fellow mobsters as the guilty parties.

Who were these suspects? Did Lucky Luciano have a slew of hits put out on enemies after the horrific beating he endured? A woman's shoe prints in the sand? More twists and turns make this the most debated and diverse mysteries of Luciano's entire life. Luciano's survival and scars, regardless of how these were achieved, gave an immeasurable boost to the gangster's street credibility. By the time the incident had faded from the news, both his enemies and law enforcement viewed Lucky Luciano as someone who now walked with an air of invincibility. Lucky was preparing to exercise this newfound reverence by enlisting a virtual army of multi-cultural mobsters to shatter everything that was considered old school Mafioso.

CHAPTER FIVE

KILLING THEM LOUDLY

GANGLAND VIOLENCE... SEEMS a morbid but natural attribute of a criminal underworld. Why, though, do gangsters have to carry out so much physical harm? One of the reasons organized crime attracts law enforcement's attention is the violent nature innate to the core of what gangsterism is. Violence is how the bosses kept order, enforced the rules, and sometimes... for hostile takeover. There was a lot of it going on during the life and crimes of Lucky Luciano. Beatings, torture, and murder. These things didn't begin with Luciano, nor did they end with his legacy, but the violence that occurred throughout his reign certainly had a few noteworthy and mysterious moments. And, a big question... *Did Charlie ever kill anyone himself?* We'll get to that too!

The following are the three most prominent examples of violent resolve that Luciano likely had involvement:

1931 – Joe "The Boss" Masseria is gunned down in the Nuova Villa Tammaro restaurant, Coney Island, New York, April 15.

Luciano was allegedly with him, but excused himself to men's room just before the shooters entered.

1931 – Salvatore Maranzano – Shot and stabbed repeatedly buy four attackers impersonating as "tax men" in his Manhattan office, September 10. Maranzano was actually waiting for Mad Dog Coll to arrive at the time– the killer he hired to murder Luciano and Vito Genovese. Lucky and his allies knew of the plan, through Tommy Lucchese, and struck first. Coll supposedly arrived after the murder took place and simply left upon finding out what happened - happy he got half the money up front anyway and didn't have to do the job after all.

1935 – Arthur "Dutch Schultz" Flegenheimer and four associates are gunned down while dining in the Palace Chop House, Newark, New Jersey, October 24. Schultz allegedly told Luciano and the other commission bosses he would personally kill Special Prosecutor Thomas E. Dewey at some point, so the bosses decided to have Schultz knocked off before he could carry the act out. Furthermore, the commission was very interested in taking over Schultz's rackets.

There is little doubt about Luciano's role in two most ambitious murder plots ever carried out in the American underworld: Joe The Boss Masseria and Salvatore Maranzano, both assassinated in 1931. His desire to unify gangsters from various ethnicities and destroy "old world" structure was underscored by a practical understanding that his days were numbered unless action was taken. No guarantees in the underworld culture, and Lucky knew even his own employer could turn on him. To that end, he was playing both sides like a double agent. Very dangerous games indeed!

There is no mystery on the surface. Luciano successfully over-threw the primary ruling class of criminal overlords in New York City. It was deliberate, violent and meant to send a very clear message to all those aligned with the old school leadership – a brand new day was here, so get on board or be eliminated. Bring-ing an end to the so-called Castellammarese War, fought be-tween Masseria and Maranzano, also served as a turning point is what we know as *The Mafia*. It can't be stated enough – Luciano did not subscribe to the Capo Di Tutti Capi, or Boss of all Bosses system as used in the mafia. Nor did Luciano believe in an all-Si-cilian system. This is the difference between *mafia* and *the mob*. Lucky Luciano and his companions were mobsters, not Mafiosi.

And how he plotted the destruction of those old world ideals was with violent resolve. There are, however, several theories re-garding who exactly made up the hit squads that actually carried out the deadly deeds.

A logical idea would have been to employ the services of cut-throats that neither boss would easily recognize, thus eliminating the suggestion that anyone on Masseria or Maranzano's payrolls would have been present at either murder scene. It's possible of course, but unlikely. It was risky enough for Luciano himself to have been present with Masseria, but that was possibly the only way he could be sure to get the boss in a deadly spot. Some re-ports never made mention of Luciano being at the restaurant, though he was one of the first people brought in for police ques-tioning.

Nevertheless, the most commonly suggested triggermen were Vito Genovese, Joe Adonis, Bugsy Siegel and Albert "The Mad Hatter" Anastasia. Genovese and Adonis were most certainly familiar to Masseria – they were his employees, and therefore seems unlikely they would be present. However, considering the

Masseria hit was a very quick in and out raid type of murder –
perhaps it didn't really matter who was there after all. Luciano
was even thought of as possible gunslinger, but most records of
the event maintain he was in the men's room when the shooting
took place.

Arthur Nash, author of *New York City Gangland,* suggests a
very good probability - Jewish gangsters. "There's a lot of speculation but it's fairly certain Luciano would have gone with the
guys he was closest to at the time so you're talking about the Bug
& Meyer mob and so on." Nash thinks Samuel "Red" Levine,
who was considered one of the most reliable Jewish gangsters of
the era for carrying out deadly jobs, was also a distinct option. Joe
Masseria, nor his bodyguards, would have been acquainted with
Levine or Bugsy Siegel.

"There's also a generally credible letter written by a Manhattan
undertaker who was being shaken down by Gerardo Scarpato
whom, with his wife owned the restaurant," adds Nash of further
conspiracy. "This undertaker was called to meet Scarpato at the
restaurant the day Masseria was hit, and when he pulled up he
was met by Scarpato and Little Augie Pisano, who told him to
get lost and forget he was there. In the evening edition of the
newspaper, he read about the assassination."

Additionally, gangland rumors told of Ciro "The Artichoke
King" Terranova being the 'getaway' driver. Terranova's spiraling
underworld downfall allegedly began with this incident – a big
fiasco if the lore is true. According to legend, Siegel was dis-
mayed by Terranova's utter loss of composure during the escape
mode. The driver was unable to get the car in gear, showing visible
signs of nervous incompetence. Siegel, while cursing up a storm,
pushed Terranova out of the way and took the wheel himself.

Regardless of who carried out the bloodshed, one fact was undeniable, Joe "The Boss" Masseria was dead of multiple gunshot wounds, four to the body and one in the head. Nobody was ever prosecuted for the murder, but an end was brought to the Castellammarese War that was fought between Masseria and Maranzano.

Salvatore Maranzano accepted Charlie Lucania into his new dynasty, but under no circumstances did he approve of Lucky's associations with Jewish gangsters. Furthermore, "The Boss of all Bosses," as he anointed himself, knew if Lucky was capable of taking out Masseria – the same plot could be repeated against him. For that, Maranzano was determined to remove Lucky and Vito Genovese first. So, he hired Vincent "Mad Dog" Coll to carry out the hit. Coll was paid half of the bounty up front, and was told to be at Maranzano's office on September 10, 1931. As pointed out above – Coll arrived a little too late, but wasn't upset. He simply scampered away from the scene of carnage.

What transpired in Maranzano's office is, as many of these mysteries remain, just that – a mystery. When authorities arrived, they found Maranzano with bullet wounds and his throat was slashed. The general belief is that four men arrived, posing as government or tax agents. Maranzano purportedly realized they were not legitimate and reached for a gun in his desk. A scuffle ensued; Maranzano putting up quite a fight. The hit squad shot their mark numerous times, slicing his neck for good measure.

It is also very conceivable that the men were Jewish gangsters, Benjamin "Bugsy" Siegel among them. Luciano took advice from Meyer Lansky, good advice, and probably knew the benefit of having a deadly crew of men that Maranzano would not likely recognize. Whoever entered that Manhattan office and took the life of Salvatore Maranzano will likely never be positively known, but the result of the murder firmly put Luciano and his allies in control of New York's underworld.

Next… Dutch Schultz, the Beer Baron of the Bronx, the Dutchman; he had a few names, not the least of which were *cheap, arrogant,* and *insane.* Schultz was violent, and many of his peers looked at him with disdain. There is even some argument over whether or not Schultz was a member of the ruling Commission, or just a boss with some territory to rule over.

In an effort to extend his rackets, Schultz employed force to take over much of the African-American controlled Harlem territory. Stephanie St. Claire, aka Queenie or Madame St. Claire, had ruled the area. She operated the largest numbers racket in Harlem (estimated worth of $300,000, according to a 1932 newspaper report), and employed the feared and respected Ellsworth "Bumpy" Johnson to handle the enforcement and protection. St. Claire was not a person to be pushed around – not even by a mob-backed goon like Dutch Schultz. St. Clair and Bumpy Johnson tried to keep Schultz's takeover plans at bay. She reported him, took out ads against him and even put a curse on him.

The Dutchman was powerful in his own right though and did make life difficult for St. Clair – for a little while. Once Schultz began feeling the heat from the office of Thomas E. Dewey, his focus shifted to finding a way to get the law off his back. Schultz's solution – kill Dewey. There are however rules in the mob, at least back then, whereby murder of law enforcement or press was a big no-no. Well, Schultz didn't much care what the ruling body of crime thought and he openly declared war on Dewey. That move earned him a ticket to the afterlife, but not immediately.

Schultz survived the gunshot wounds, lingering in a hospital bed for several days. According to newspapers, as he lay dying – a message arrived from Queenie. It read, "As ye sow so shall ye reap." St. Clair was one of the very few numbers policy bankers who Dutch was unable to overtake, and she was reveling in the karma.

Some reports stated that Schultz never once mentioned his killers. Others, however, told of his vague ramblings, asserting two prominent mobsters were behind hit. He allegedly told investigators "The Boss" did it (police took this to mean Luciano). Yet another delirious statement implicated "John"(Torrio) and "Chink" (Charles Sherman). Both Luciano and Torrio were conveniently "resting" in Miami at the time of Dutch's assault.

Interestingly, knocking Dutch off was not the end of the violence. Even some of Dutch's own enemies were then brutally wiped out. One particularly gruesome example was that of the Schultz implicated "Chink." Charles "Chink" Sherman, a Broadway nightclub operator, was known as a bitter Schultz enemy (dating back to 1931 when he survived being shot and slashed in a fight with the Dutchman's boys). Several days after the attack on Schultz, Sherman was kidnapped from the front of his club. Forty-eight hours later, his body was discovered in a pit of quicklime – he had been hacked to death with an axe. The killers intentionally balled his hand up into a fist, so to protect his fingerprints for later identification. This was one of many gangland murders, eight in total the press reported, since the assassination of Dutch Schultz and his associates.

As for Queenie and Bumpy, legend states they were given back control of the Harlem numbers racket, by Lucky Luciano's decision, on the condition they pay the "tax" as all others were obligated. Bumpy became quite a folk hero in Harlem, eventually handling enforcement and narcotics work for the Genovese Family in later years. Queenie made the news only a handful of times after 1935; Bumpy was often under scrutiny for narcotics, and served time in Alcatraz.

So these were the most notorious 'hits of which Luciano was linked, but there is an even greater mystery: *Did Lucky Luciano ever commit a murder himself?*

Definitively speaking – we may never know. Luciano had not discussed, in any recorded detail, the hits he ordered nor any he may have actually carried out himself. All those who may have been privy to such information are also long gone now, and so are their secrets. Lucky once answered an interview question regarding knowledge of Dutch Schultz's killing, "Maybe I know something about it. Maybe I don't want to talk about it." That was about the extent of his 'admission' to any role in murder. And even with that, Luciano did not physically kill Schultz (Charles "The Bug" Workman of *Murder Inc.* was convicted of the crime).

Nonetheless, author Tim Newark pointed out a very distinct possibility of Luciano's killer instinct in his book *Boardwalk Gangster: The Real Lucky Luciano*. According to the theory – Luciano may have indeed been the ice-cold gunman to take down one of Joe "The Boss" Masseria's mortal enemies. And here's how it played out...

By 1922, Umberto Valenti was, according to police at the time, responsible for more 'hits' than any other man in the city. One of his primary targets, the rival he personally wanted to exterminate, was Joe Masseria. Valenti, along with an entourage of would-be killers, caught Masseria off guard, fired several shots from almost point blank range, and completely missed the mark, save for two bullet holes in Masseria's hat. Six others were wounded in the battle. The incident at Second Avenue ultimately achieved two things: Masseria became even more 'immortal' in his own mind and it sealed the inevitable death warrant for Valenti.

Just a few days later, gunfire erupted again in the Second Avenue vicinity. This time, however, the tables were turned on Valenti. It was 11:45 am on August 11, 1922 – people going about their daily business crowded the corner of Second Avenue and 12th Street. Umberto Valenti and a few of his men were there too.

As Valenti looked around, he saw several men approaching, each brandishing revolvers. He must've known immediately his life was in great danger; he ran quickly into the street toward a taxicab, while his associates ran in other directions. Before he could enter the cab, shots rang out. The gunmen were, according to witnesses, firing wildly. This was just the sort of violence that police, citizens and government officials were becoming exceedingly disgusted with. Besides the gang on gang bloodshed, again there was collateral damage. street sweeper Joseph Shepis, age 42, was hit in the neck and an eleven-year-old (some reports identified her as eight years old) girl, Agnes Egglinger, visiting from New Haven, Connecticut, was hit in chest – the bullet lodging in her arm.

Valenti tried to return fire, but it was all in vain. He dropped his weapon. Amidst all the chaos, taxi driver Samuel Zuckenberg had no idea that the man was about to be murdered.

Witnesses said one gunman of the lot remained cold, calculated and unrelenting... aiming carefully, undeterred by the ensuing chaos. The rounds hit Valenti in the chest, just shy of his heart.

"It was the coolest thing I ever saw," nineteen-years-old witness Jack Kahane said. "People were shrieking and running in all directions, and this fellow calmly fired shot after shot. He did not move until he emptied his weapon."

The man who shot Valenti was described as svelte, swarthy complexion, dark hair, and like the other perpetrators – well dressed. And this slender cold-blooded killer ran into the alleyways, evading capture by bystanders and police. Valenti died of his wounds in St. Marks Hospital and police subsequently questioned only Joe Masseria.

Was Umberto Valenti's killer Lucky Luciano? Could've been. The physical description fit the young Luciano, and he knew the area extremely well – well enough to escape a large crowd and cops alike. Furthermore, Lucky was looking to earn a higher rank in Masseria's organization, this would have been the golden ticket.

The only other recorded cases of Luciano's literal involvement in a shooting were two instances of *attempted* murder. First, the 1926 assault of Albert Levy and his chauffeur Charles Haffman. Leading up to the assault, police had become increasingly concerned about a "war" between East and Westside gangs, fighting over the "spoils" from protection rackets, particularly the protection of gambling establishments. From the West – the Diamond Brothers gang, led by "Legs" and included brother Ed, Thomas "Fatty" Walsh (newspaper report of arrest identified him as *James* Walsh) and Salvatore Lucania.

It was of little surprise to police then, when after a car on car shooting took place in the vicinity of Broadway, that the Diamond crew was named. Levy, an insurance broker, said he was carrying $8000 while Haffman drove him home from a dinner. A car approached, someone from inside demanded money, but Haffman tried to evade the robbers. Four men, Levy told police, exited a vehicle – firing shots – some of which hit Levy. A nearby patrolman helped thwart the attack, but the perpetrators escaped the scene.

Cops later grabbed the four suspects in for questioning, and brought two of them before Levy in his hospital room. The insurance broker suddenly refused to press charges, saying they were the wrong men. Police were confident the Diamond Gang was responsible for an attempted restaurant robbery and the ensuing gunplay against Levy, but all four were discharged in Magistrate's court. Its very likely Lucky was indeed a key figure in the shooting.

In May of 1933, police apparently had Lepke and Luciano in mind, following a full-blown gangster shootout that unfolded on Broadway, just as theatergoers were exiting the midnight shows. There's not much evidence or reporting directly linking either man to the incident, so it is truly a mystery.

Several vehicles raced through streets; occupants exchanging gunfire. Two vehicles were sandwiching a third, shooters firing into it. Three bystanders – Irene Savage, Sadie Fortine and Walter O' Donald – were hit by bullets; Savage in the shoulder, Fortine in the back and O' Donald grazed on the forehead. The targeted car was found abandoned a few blocks away. The occupants had escaped, but police discovered blood smeared in the back seat, the vehicle body riddled with bullet holes. Witnesses saw two men limping, with a trail of blood into the darkness.

"No small timer owned this car," a detective said after noticing the vehicle was reinforced with inch thick glass, special padding and a steel reinforced roof.

Why did police suspect Lepke and Luciano were involved? Possibly because, it was presumed at first, that some of the individuals mixed up in this mess were loyal to Waxey Gordon – a rival of Luciano, Lansky and Lepke. Gordon – real name Irving Wexler – took over the late Arnold Rothstein's bootlegging business. Though he was once allied with Luciano, an unofficial gang war ensued over the liquor business, specifically between Lansky and Gordon.

The bad blood, gangland grapevine says, led to Luciano and Lansky supplying prosecutors with information that put Gordon away for ten years. Then, in September, three men were questioned in connection with the gunfight – all notable associates of Waxey – "Chink" Sherman, his brother Henry and Jack Weinstein. All had been in custody on weapons and narcotics charges (dropped for lack of evidence), but police figured on holding the men on Felonious Assault charges for the injuries on the bystanders. All three denied involvement.

The interesting part of the story, however, was the connection investigators told the press regarding a "beer war" and the men behind it. Buchalter and Luciano, the report stated, were in a the war with Gordon, but "has been ended by a truce."

Though possible, it is highly unlikely that Lepke and Lucky physically engaged in a gun battle on Broadway with Waxey's men. Enlisted mob gunslingers; not Lepke and Lucky, who were bosses on the Commission, probably carried out the job. Police and media reports were elusive, but it seems they knew where the orders for such violence were originating, and that is just as criminal as pulling the trigger.

** Realistically, after 1931, most Syndicate sanctioned killings would have been carried out by a specific team of individuals, dubbed "*Murder Inc.*" by the media. The unit was based in a candy shop called Midnight Roses. Member included; Harry "Pittsburgh Phil" Strauss, Harry "Happy" Maione, Frank "The Dasher" Abbandando, Seymour "Blue Jaw" Magoon, Albert "Tick Tock" Tannenbaum, Martin "Bugsy" Goldstein, Louis Capone (no relation to Al), Charles "The Bug" Workman and others. The top boss was Louis "Lepke" Buchalter. Under boss roles were filled by Albert Anastasia and Abe "Kid Twist" Reles. (Some believe Bugsy Siegel and Joe Adonis were instrumental in the formation of Murder Inc.)

CHAPTER SIX

VERY BAD MEN

JUST A MONTH following the murder of "Boss of all Bosses" Salvatore Maranzano, another crucial moment in the evolution of the National Crime Syndicate took place. This, essentially, was an incident that not only officially inaugurated the Italian – Jewish unification that Luciano and Meyer Lansky desired, but also brought a controversial law into question.

It all began from complaints, by the Amalgamated Clothing Workers' Union, that racketeers were "terrorizing" the industry. New York Mayor Jimmy Walker was inundated with the union request to clean up the gangster element. Union President Sidney Hillman, also had names of a few racketeers he wanted police to put the squeeze on. So, the Mayor gave Police Commissioner Mulrooney the *go ahead* to crack down. The officials were armed with the power of a statute, that was piggy backed to a Disorderly Conduct law. "Public Enemy" law, was broadly designed to give authorities the green light to, on their judgment, apprehend known criminals – when they were *consorting together*.

On the night of November 10th, 1931, a team of ten detectives, led by Assistant Chief Inspector John J. Sullivan and Inspector John J. Lyons, paid a visit the Hotel Franconia on West Seventy-Second Street in Manhattan. They were operating from information provided by Mayor Walker, the Union President Sidney Hillman and subordinate officers within the police force (who had been keeping some of the suspects under surveillance for weeks). The information provided made them aware a gathering of mobsters was taking place in a suite located in the Franconia (owned by the late Arnold Rothstein). Police weren't certain how many alleged racketeers were in the suite, but they were sure, at the very least, one primary target was there – Louise "Lepke" Buchalter.

Detectives from the "Radical Squad" descended on the suspected hotel suite, which was registered under the name "Rosen", at 6 pm and remained there until 3 am. according to another officer present during the raid, Lieutenant James Pike of Criminal Alien Squad, a garment union representative named Max Rubin called the hotel room – adding more damning evidence (later used as testimony against the men arrested.)

The alleged racketeers were taken to police headquarters for processing. The nine defendants were listed as (most of their names and nicknames were misspelled in various ways, from one news report to the next); Benjamin (Bugsy) Siegel, Louis (Lepke) Buckhouse, Harry Greenberg, Hyman Holtz, Jacob Shapiro, Joseph Rosen, Louis Kravitz (aka Louis Kay – who became a fugitive in 1937 following accusations of being in charge of Lepke's narcotics racket), Philip Kavalich, and Henry (Harry) Teitelbaum (who had physically rented the suite under the name Rosen.)

The law by which the nine men were arrested had been controversial since its inception and *only* implemented as a "temporary" solution during an investigation known as the Hofstadter legislative inquiry. "Consorting Together" – is how the allegation was termed, but the groups' lawyer promptly asked the courts for a dismissal of the charge, because the law was enacted during an emergency session and not for use outside of the circumstances from the Hofstadter inquiry. The request was denied, but attorney Samuel Liebowitz took the case before Magistrate Gottleib.

Leibowitz presented his case for Gottleib to consider. No decision was immediately made, and Gottleib adjourned court for a few days. However, one of the nine gangsters – Jacob Shapiro – was served with a deportation warrant as he was leaving court.

Shapiro had a lengthy criminal record, which was the foundation of the government's plans to deport him. In particular, Shapiro was involved in a 1929 murder of Augie Orgen, and the injury of Jack "Legs" Diamond – who was acting as Orgen's bodyguard. Shapiro was discharged in the case, but authorities were sure to make the connection public information, especially since Louis "Lepke" Buchalter had also been implicated in the Orgen murder case. Furthermore, and in direct relation to the clothing industry issue, Shapiro, Buchalter and Louis Kravitz were three of five men apprehended in 1929 following the destruction of M. & L. Rosenblatt clothing company on Broadway.

Court reconvened several days later, and Gottleib was getting an earful from Police Commissioner Mulrooney.

"They are known as criminals and racketeers, men who exercised influence in gangland, capable of homicide or sabotage," Mulrooney proclaimed.

The commissioner was rightfully concerned the nine gangsters might get a free pass. Magistrate Gottleib had a reputation for empathy, known for exercising fairness and leniency on petty crimes (his obituary in 1933 read "noted for his charitable attitude toward petty crimes induced by poverty, and founder of the Bricken Fund for making small loans to the poor.") Assistant District Attorney Robert Daru tried to convince the Magistrate, imploring the entire case was built around the men being of "evil reputation."

Mulrooney contended that three of the accused were "known criminals" – Shapiro, Buchalter and Holtz. However, he also admitted he personally couldn't recognize any of them himself, but based in his belief on the reputation the men had within the larger police force. Adding to the case against the gangsters, virtually every police officer that took the stand called the men, "Very bad." Also in an attempt to prove the prosecutions accusations, fingers were pointed at Benjamin "Bugsy" Siegel. Detectives present on the Franconia raid had also identified a Lincoln parked outside, complete with bulletproof glass and reinforced body– belonging to Siegel.

During the 1920s and 30s, especially in cities with heavy underworld activity, it was not unusual for police and the public to presume those driving decked out bullet proof vehicles were indeed gangsters. However, the question before Magistrate Gottleib was far beyond what these men were driving expensive vehicles, or why they were having a meeting in an expensive hotel suite. The ultimate issue was the *legality* of the law they had been in violation of.

The defense also had witnesses, specifically to refute the "very bad" label prosecutors placed on their clients. One such witness was James Reardon, the Vice President of the United States Trucking Corporation. Reardon told the court Siegel worked for him from 1917 to 1921 and was of good character. Prosecutor

Daru, who had categorized eight of the nine men as "of evil character," asked Reardon if his opinion would change, based on the fact Siegel had an arrest record.

"As far as I know," Reardon replied, "He's all right. I'd give him a job any day."

On December 24th, 1931, all nine of the Jewish men received a Christmas gift. Magistrate Maurice Gottleib discharged all them. His decision was based solely on one important fact: the Public Enemy amendment to the Disorderly Conduct law was only an emergency decision, which expired in March of 1931 anyway. Gottleib explained that the police simply had not proved the men had assembled for unlawful purpose.

"There was not the slightest evidence presented by the State in this case to show these defendant had met unlawfully," Gottleib declared.

However, the Magistrate was not about to criticize the police for carrying out their duties, and by no means did he believe the defendants were saints of any kind. His decision was not based on anything but how the law itself was to be interpreted.

"I have no doubt that all but one of the defendants are men of evil character and a liability on the community," continued Gottleib. "If it were not for the face the 'unlawful purpose' element in the charge against them had not been proved, I would not hesitate to sentence them to the full penalty."

He closed the session with one final thought: "All law primarily is concerned with the rules of conduct, whether the conduct be of the good or evil minded. I cannot understand why this law had been limited if intended as a temporary means to combat the growing gangster evil. There is only one rule of evidence. We cannot construe testimony in one manner for the criminal and have another construction for the citizen of good intention."

With that, all nine men were released. Commissioner Mulrooney maintained that at least three of the newly freed men were a "danger to the community."

The mystery remained though… why were nine known gangsters meeting in the first place? Well, if underworld folklore and reasonable assumptions were on the right track, then it would be very likely the men were meeting on the request of Meyer Lansky. Only two months had passed since Jewish gangsters, sanctioned by Lucky Luciano and Meyer Lansky, killed Salvatore Maranzano, presumably. The next phase of development for a truly organized and unified crime empire was to make sure everyone was on board. Luciano had a long list of Italian gangsters loyal to his cause. Lansky then, as the story goes, asked Bugsy Siegel to explain how things were going to work from now on, essentially bringing the Jewish faction into the fray. So there it happened – the next steps in what would become the most prolific criminal enterprise of the twentieth century. The meeting was quite possibly a trifecta – the birth a unified mob, the pre-formation of the mob's enforcement arm (Murder Inc.) and in the process, law and order were put to the test (ironically, the Public Enemy law was further strengthened by 1935).

1926
Salvatore Lucania aka Lucky Luciano before he was scarred.
Lucky was arrested along with the Irish gangsters Jack Legs Diamond, Ed Diamond &
Fatty Walsh for the assault of an insurance salesman.
(C. Cipollini Collection)

1926
Police Lineup of Diamond Brothers Gang
L to R:
Ed Diamond, Jack Diamond,Thomas Walsh, Salvatore Lucania
(C. Jones Collection)

1928
Park Central Hotel
Scene of Arnold Rothstein Murder
(C. Cipollini Collection)

1928
Arnold Rothstein
Gambler, Narcotics Financier & mentor to many up and coming mobsters, such as Lucky
Luciano, Meyer Lansky, Legs Diamond, Frank Erickson and George Uffner.
(C. Jones Collection)

1929
Thomas "Fatty" Walsh & Arthur L. Clark
Walsh was murderd, Clark injured at the Miami Biltmore Hotel.
Though never solved, the crime was considered in relation to Walsh's previous business
relationship with the slain Arnold Rothstein.
(C. Cipollini Collection)

1929
Charles Lucania
Beaten, bruised, left for dead on Hylan Boulevard.
Sketch by Natasha Cipollini

1929
Alphonse "Scarface" Capone
(C. Jones Collection)

1929
Police remove bodies of slain gangsters from the St. Valentine's Day Massacre scene.
(C. Cipollini Collection)

1929
Coroner swears in jurors in probe of St. Valentine's Day Massacre in Chicago. The
bodies of seven dead are on display.
(C. Jones Collection)

MASSERIA-MARANZANO WAR AND EVOLUTION OF GANG CONTROL-1930 TO PRESENT

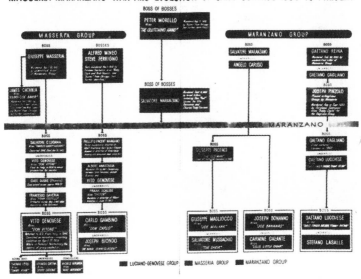

1963
McLellan Hearings Chart
Heirarchy of Castellammarese War- Salvatore Lucania aka Lucky Luciano shown under
Masseria's group.
(C. Cipollini Collection)

1931
Charles "Lucky" Luciano
The year he orchestrated the murders of both warring New York Mafia bosses - Joe
Masseria & Salvatore Maranzano
(C. Cipollini Collection)

1931

On November 10th, nine Jewish gangsters were arrested at Arnold Rothstein's Hotel Franconia under a bizarre statute allowing authorities to round up "known" criminals that are congregating. Among those arrested were Joseph Rosen, Benjamin "Bugsy" Siegel, Harry Teitelbaum, Harry Greenberg (Harry Schachter) and Louis "Lepke" Buchalter. One legend states the men were meeting so Bugsy could inform the others that they were all now working in alliance with Luciano and the Italian mobsters. This was also possibly the early stages of the mob's enforcement division - Murder Inc. (C. Cipollini Collection)

September 10, 1931
Salvatore Maranzano
Crime Scene
Maranzano was assassinated in his office by Luciano henchmen disguised as tax men. Lucky made the move after hearing Maranzanzo put a hit out on him first.
(Crime Scene Photo)

April 15, 1931
Joe "The Boss" Masseria
Crime Scene
Masseria was shot dead by gunmen after Luciano excused himself to the men's room.
(Crime Scene Photo)

1931
The Irish gangster Jack "Legs" Diamond reaches almost folk hero status, surviving
numerous assasination attempts. A year before, Legs, along with Lucky and a few other
men, tried to secure a European narcotics pipeline.
(C. Cipollini Collection)

1932
L to R: Paul "The Waiter" Ricca, Salvatore Agoglia, Charlie 'Lucky' Luciano, Meyer
Lansky, John Senna, Harry Brown Lucky and Meyer were arrested in Chicago while on
visit with Al Capone's "Outfit" entourage.
(C. Cipollini Collection)

1937
Chief Assistant District Attorney Thomas Dewey and Mayor Fiorello LaGuardia
The pair would make many headlines, individually and together, as the mob busters.
The Luciano case of 1936 would be Dewey's claim to fame.
(C. Jones Collection)

1937
Madame Stephanie St. Clair
Queen of Harlem Numbers Racket

1953
Ellsworth "Bumpy" Johnson
Enforcer & Kingpin

(Photos: Washington Afro-American)

1942
Policy Racket
Common types of betting slips.
(C. Cipollini Collection)

Mobster Dutch Schultz muscled in on St. Clair's Harlem rackets, but she and Bumpy
fought back. When Schultz told Luciano and the Commission bosses he was going to
kill Prosecutor Thomas E. Dewey in 1935 - the bosses struck first, having Murder Inc.
assassins take Schultz out. Before he died in the hospital, St. Clair sent him a message
reading, "Legends tell of Luciano giving the Harlem rackets back to St. Clair in return for
a 'tax' paid to the Syndicate."
(C. Jones Collection)

1939
John "The Fox" Torrio
Once Al Capone's mentor, The Fox 'retired' and returned to New York where he was instrumental in The Seven Group and the assasination of Dutch Schultz. He and Luciano remained very close confidants as the reformation of the mob syndicate was developing from 1931 through Lucky's incarceration in 1936.
(C. Cipollini Collection)

Newspaper notation pasted to back of a Luciano mugshot photo mentions one of the more bizarre theories behind Lucky's scars.
(C. Cipollini Collection)

1935
Actress Thelma Todd was found dead in her driveway.
Rumors circulated for decades that her death was suspicious, including theories that Luciano was behind it.
(Crime Scene Photo)

1936
Lucky Luciano (covering face in disbelief) arrives at police headquarters in New York.
He was extradited from Arkansas under heavy police guard and processed on April 18th.
Lucky claimed police had "kidnapped" him from Hot Springs and was "Sore as Hell" at
the vice charges brought against him by Thomas E. Dewey.
(C. Cipollini Collection)

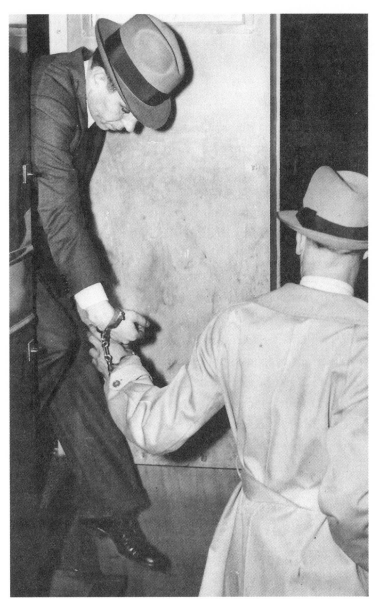

1936
Charles "Lucky" Luciano
Cuffed to a detective, exiting a "Black Maria" (paddy wagon) and headed into Supreme Court for sentencing.
(C. Cipollini Collection)

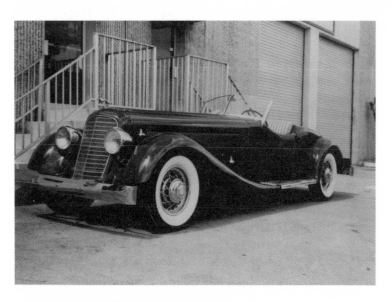

Luciano's Custom 1936 Packard V-12
(C. Cipollini Collection)

1936
Luciano leaves Supreme Court on June
18th, following sentencing of 30 to 50
years by Judge Phillip J. McCook.
(C. Cipollini Collection)

1936
Escorted by detectives, twelve jurors enter court to deliberate the fate of Luciano and
his co-defendants.
(C. Cipollini Collection)

1936
Jack Eller and Charles "Lucky" Luciano
Escorted by detectives, the pair enter Sing Sing Prison.
The unknown woman on the right ran past guards and quickly kissed one of the two prisoners just moments after this photo was taken. *Unfortunately the press did not specify which one got the kiss.
(C. Cipollini Collection)

1937
Galina Orloff aka Gay Orlova
Luciano's showgirl love interest from early 1935 through his 1936 conviction.
(C. Jones Collection)

1934
Gay Orlova
Blonde Broadway Starlet

1934
Gay Orlova Meets Lucky Luciano in Miami
during a special New Years Eve run of
Earl Carroll's Show.
(The Miami News)

Gay Orlova
Cover of LAFF Magazine
(C. Cipollini Collection)

1936
Joe Silvers (center) & Leo Maimone (covering face)
The pair were arrested in New York, brought to Washington D.C. & later freed by
authorities following Jean Bell's failure to identify them as her alleged attackers.
(C. Cipollini Collection)

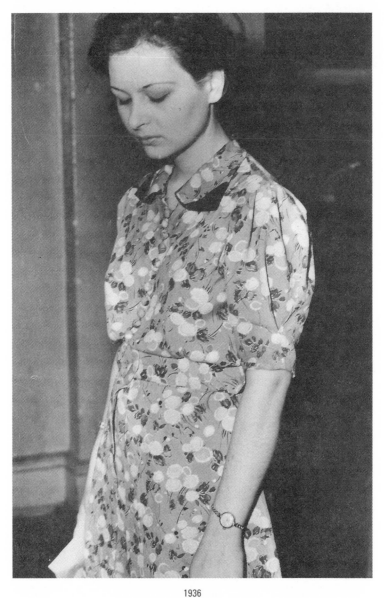

1936
Margaret Louise Bell aka Jean Bell
The 23 year old redhead claimed goons carved Luciano's initials into her thigh and
numbers into her abdomen.
Police eventually discovered she had a history of aliases and false police reports. The
final ruling was Bell inflicted the wounds herself.
(C. Cipollini Collection)

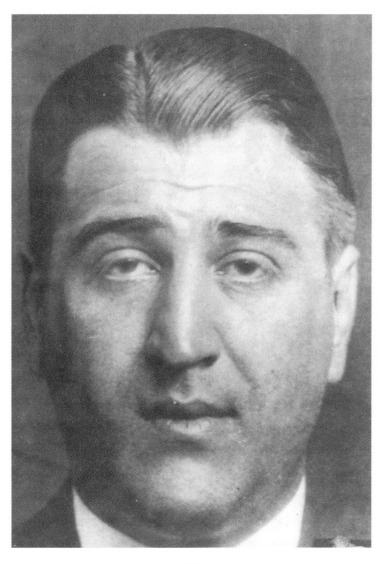

1936
Leo Maimone
A known gangster dating back to at least 1926 when, after a vthwarted robbery attempt,
he was shot in the wrist while scuffling with police..
(C. Cipollini Collection)

1959
Frank Erickson
Millionaire Bookie & Original Gangster
associate of Luciano, Uffner, Lansky,
Costello and Rothstein.
(C. Cipollini Collection)

1941
Enoch "Nucky" Johnson
He hosted the 1929 gangland convention in
Atlantic City.
(C. Cipollini Collection)

1937
Joe Adonis
Some legends state he was a member of
the hit squad that murdered Joe "The Boss"
Masseria in 1931. He voluntarily deported
himself to Italy in 1956 to avoid prosecution
for a perjury charge. It is not known if he
ever tried to visit with Luciano while the two
were in exile.
(C. Cipollini Collection)

1940
Albert "Tick Tock" Tannenbaum & Abe "Kid Twist" Reles
The enforcement arm of the National Crime Syndicate was dubbed "Murder Inc." by
the media. Two of the top members of the murdering group turned witness, almost
completely destroying the most deadly crew of hired assassins in underworld history.
Murder Inc. (aka Ocean Hill/Brownsville Combination) was comprised primarily of
Jewish and Italian gangsters. The boss in charge was Louis "Lepke" Buchalter, with
direct bosses being Reles and Albert Anastasia. Some of the killers went to the electric
chair, including Lepke - the only top crime boss to ever be executed.
(C. Cipollini Collection)

1942
Attorney Jerry Gleisman congratulates Benjamin "Bugsy" Siegel after an acquittal in the murder case of fellow gangster Harry Greenberg.
(C. Cipollini Collection)

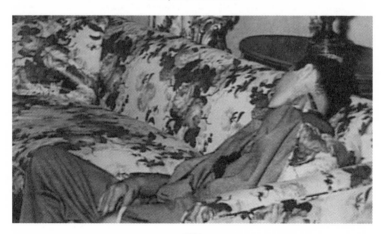

1947
Benjamin "Bugsy" Siegel
Shot to death while reading the newspaper in girlfriend Virginia Hill's California home.
(Crime Scene Photo)

1941
Beverly Paterno
The socialite, or Cafe Society girl as the press called her, met Luciano in Havana during
the 'crime conference' of 1946 & began a brief but highly publicized affair with him.
(C. Cipollini Collection)

1947
Luciano's Mansion
30th Street, near 5th Avenue, Miramar Cuba
(C. Cipollini Collection)

1947
From Left to Right:
Benito Herrera (Chief of Secret Police), Charles "Lucky" Luciano, Alfredo Pequeno
(Cuban Minister of Interior).
Lucky was arrested in a cafe on March 7th to face deportation from Cuba back to Italy.
(C. Cipollini Collection)

1947
Lucky Luciano is arrested while staying in
Havana Cuba.
Cuba is put under pressure of sanctions by
the United States to kick Lucky out.
(C. Cipollini Collection)

1949
Despite being upset at exile to Italy from
both the United States and Cuba, Luciano
manages to share a laugh with friends.
(C. Cipollini Collection)

1949
Luciano partying in Rome.
(C. Jones Collection)

1958
Meyer Lansky
Considered the kingpin of gambling in Cuba,
he is questioned by police during a visit to
New York regarding the murder of Albert "The
Mad Hatter" Anastasia the previous year.
(C. Cipollini Collection)

1949
Igea Lissoni
The former ballerina was quite possibly
the one true love in Lucky Luciano's Life.
(C. Cipollini Collection)

1959
Donald Byington
Former prison guard turned Warden had experiences with gangsters including; Louis "Lepke" Buchalter, Jack "Legs" Diamond and Al Capone. The one he found most memorable was Luciano. "If I had to pick the most dangerous person," Byington told the press in 1981, "It was Luciano."
(C. Cipollini Collection)

1955
Charles "Lucky" Luciano with "Bombi" the dog in Naples.
He had two loves - his pets and his girlfriend Igea Lissoni, but authorities believed his real love was the money earned from an international narcotics racket.
(C. Cipollini Collection)

1962
Henry A. Blanke
Retired Detective was a young patrolman
when he found & rescued a bloodied
Lucky Luciano crawling along a Staten
Island road in October 1929.
(Sarasota Herald-Tribune)

1962
Actor Cameron Mitchell and Charles "Lucky" Luciano
Mitchell and his family endured numerous threats after agreeing to play the role of
Luciano in a purposed film version to be produced by Martin Gosch.
(C. Cipollini Collection)

(Undated Photo)
George Uffner
During the investigation of Arnold
Rothstein's murder in 1928, Uffner, Fatty
Walsh and Lucky Luciano were taken in
for questioning. All were released, but
suspicions lingered the trio had intimate
knowledge of the crime.
(Courtesy of family source)

George Uffner & Evelyn Carmel
(Courtesy of Family Source)

1951
Frank Costello
"Prime Minister of the Underworld"
Always good for the cameras, he gives a panhandler some change outside courthouse.
(C. Cipollini Collection)

1961
Lucky Luciano & Adriana Rizzo
(Rizzo's personal snapshots appeared in Parade
Magazine in 1962)

1961
Adriana Rizzo, Lucky Luciano, and unidentied woman pose at beach.
(Rizzo's personal snapshots appeared in Parade Magazine in 1962)

1936
Charles "Lucky" Luciano
Perhaps the most iconic and widely recognized photograph of the infamous gangster.
(C. Cipollini Collection)

CHAPTER SEVEN

SEX, LIES AND SUICIDE

LUCKY LUCIANO'S VISION of a *national crime syndicate* was being fully realized by the end of 1931. His companions in crime convened at the newly formed "board", among them Meyer Lansky, Louis "Lepke" Buchalter, Benjamin "Bugsy" Siegel, and Frank Costello, enjoying the unification of forces they created in the wake of carrying out the murders of Joe "The Boss" Masseria and Salvatore Maranzano just a year before. Although Luciano is often thought of as a "Boss of all Bosses," neither he nor his colleagues subscribed to that ideology. That idea was quashed with removal of the "old school" Mafioso. This was a commission, complete with votes and meetings like any legitimate corporation would hold. Nonetheless, his power and money was growing, as was his recognition as the 'top' mobster in America. With that came other benefits for Lucky, such as the ability to charm attractive young women. However, it should be no surprise that his 'bad boy' allure would also attract some equally diabolical female followers.

The same year that Luciano's murderous removal of warring mob bosses made headlines - the first media mentions were being made of a stunning blonde showgirl, who fled the Bolshevik uprising of the Russian Revolution, here in the United States to wow theatergoers. Hers was a fascinating tale, both comedic and quite tragic. At first, she was a media darling, capturing the attention of reporters and reviewers - having brief complimentary write ups and photos for the papers became almost commonplace. Over time, she would forever be associated with the underworld's most infamous underworld leader. The latter, however, was not the worst of her ordeals.

Long before this woman met Lucky Luciano, she was caught in the whirlwind chaos of Russia's Marxist takeover. Her family fled the revolution, eventually made their way to France, and that's where young Galina Orloff picked up a love for dance and performance art. In 1929, when she was just fifteen years old, her mother then moved her to New York. A 'student' visa approved her stay in the States, but Orloff was not in pursuit of an education. She had known exactly what she wanted out of the Big Apple.

By age eighteen, Orloff landed a spot on Broadway. She had already changed her name to a more 'showbiz suitable' moniker. On the suggestion of others, reportedly a male admirer, Galina Orloff became *Gay Orlova*. The name change, along with her unmistakable good looks worked to her benefit. Soon, Orlova secured a spot on the showbiz circuit – she became a *Vanities* girl. It was said producer Earl Carroll spotted her in a casting call filled with many other big dreamers hoping to land a role – she stood out to him. At that moment the dancer, whose name eventually would forever be associated with America's most notorious gangster, wanted nothing more than to live the high life, and perform on Broadway.

Charles Luciano was a frequent visitor of Broadway haunts. From restaurants to shows, he was a recognizable character in both the underworld and legitimate nightlife circles. Police and reporters often called him a "Broadway Racketeer." He liked the showgirls and striptease artists; they were often drawn to his power and charisma. Gay was young, impressionable, enthralled by the upscale lifestyles, yet had lived (and was living) years ahead of her actual age. Fate or coincidence, Charlie and Gay were going to meet – but oddly enough – not in New York City.

Orlova never had a top-billed role in Carroll's shows, but again, she always garnered notice from photographers and theatre critics (it should also be noted her name was often the subject of both compliment and parody, as theatre and gossip writers were either bemused or titillated by Broadway dancers' stage name choices.) She, as Carroll felt upon meeting her the first time, did have that 'something' that seemed to magnetically draw in those who spotted her. Plus, Gay was sarcastic, sharp tongued – and known for downing champagne and smoking expensive cigars with the best of them. She was a noticeable character indeed.

Orlova appeared in two of Carroll's New York based shows before jaunting off to France in the early part of 1933. While there, performing risqué fan dance to Parisian audiences, she met a French nobleman and fell in love. Tales circulated that the romance quickly floundered because his aristocratic family looked down on such a relationship – a nobleman with a burlesque performer was out of the question. Not easily discouraged from following her dreams, the carefree showgirl headed back to the United States.

From fall of 1933 through spring of 1934 Orlova appeared in Earl Carroll's acclaimed *Murder at the Vanities*. The show was performed at the Majesty Theatre where a young second balcony usher named Edward W.F. Finn would often find himself mesmerized by Orlova, both on stage and off. He was just nineteen years old and earning ten dollars a week. Finn was innocent, but somewhat practical, realizing the showgirls on stage were lovers of luxury and fancy men. He was a simple man, eking out a wage and living at home with his mother. But Gay Orlova had been watching young Finn as well.

Following one of the performances of *Murder*, Finn and other ushers were among those invited back to Orlova's Brooklyn apartment. Finn had implied later that he was very much out of his element, amazed at the chance to eat caviar and rub elbows with the cast outside of work. At the party, someone told Finn about Orlova's voyeuristic peaks at him through the curtain while he worked the balcony area. He didn't think much of it though, saying "all the actors do that to see how big the house is going to be."

The following day though, Gay Orlova asked Finn and another usher to accompany her to the movies. "The night after that," said Finn, "I took her alone." The pair went swimming together, rode around town in a cab and generally hit it off very well (he admitted Orlova paid for everything). Finn was in awe and beginning to fall for the dancer. "She said I was nice looking which was something, coming from a lady with her good looks."

As the weeks passed and the pair got increasingly closer, Finn still remained a little bewildered by the whole situation. He was very cognizant of his own star struck sensation and still feeling a bit out of sorts wondering why this lovely showgirl had an eye for him. Nevertheless, the two continued to spend time together. How close? Finn implied the pair kissed and, in his words, "necked." That however was the extent of physical relations, or at least as far as Finn was willing to elaborate.

Then, Edward Finn's true sense of shock and awe arrived when Orlova bluntly suggested the two get married. The proposal was made after Finn told Gay he considered moving to Texas with a friend, a place where he thought he could get rich enough to marry a girl like her. Orlova put on a sullen face and said to him, "You'd do better to stay here and marry me." But Finn was wary. Having seen so many shows in his young life, he recalled the ones where a man is made a fool by a clever and conniving beauty. He did not want to play that role. But Orlova kept assuring him she meant it – they should wed. His other concern was money. "You move right in here with me," Orlova told him. "I have influential friends who will get you a job with big money."

To the displeasure and natural skepticism of his mother (she used the analogy of a "gold brick" to drive the point home) and even the disbelief of his pals, Edward Finn wed Gay Orlova in a brief exchange at the municipal building, in front of a few friends as witnesses. In the taxi back from the ceremony, Finn began making suggestions for how the couple should spend some time before they both have to return to the theatre for work, but Gay was quick to douse the glee of the new groom. "I'm going shopping with a girl friend, "Orlova said while handing him a ticket to the Winter Garden performance for that night. "Guess there won't be much time to see you at the theatre tonight, so we won't try. Call me up tomorrow."

Before the ink could dry on the marriage license, Orlova had plans for travel to Europe and back, leaving Finn completely stunned and alone. His own intuition, plus the warning of his mother and friends were all proving to be terribly true. What

Finn hadn't known – Orlova was still living in the United States on her student visa. Although not much trouble would be given to someone for that in and of itself, Gay wanted to travel to London (as many showgirls did from time to time) and Paris, but to get back into the States would become a problem. Marriage solved that problem; Edward Finn was merely a pawn.

Days had gone by with hardly a hello between them, though he worked the second balcony, watching his wife perform nightly. Finally she called for him and in her typically abrupt manner – handed Finn some papers and said, "Sign these, it's just formality." The documents were the last thing she needed to prove she was married to a U.S. citizen. She promised to see him in a few months; travel was still the priority on her agenda. Putting insult to injury, Finn spotted a group of workers laughing at the theatre bulletin board. The joke was on him, with a note from Earl Carroll that read: "If you had to marry an usher, why from the second balcony?" Finn was devastated.

She had told Finn her job was important and a show in London would keep her busy for several months. Just as she was about to board a steamer set for England, Finn caught up with his disappearing bride and asked what he was supposed to do now. She replied, "Get a divorce." Orlova was well aware that marriage, not divorce, determined her citizenship. And she did indeed jaunt off to exotic locations for several years while Edward Finn simply pondered his remarkably sad situation. Still, he hadn't divorced her – yet.

One of the shows Gay Orlova was booked to appear in, beyond New York's borders and far away from Edward Finn, was scheduled for New Years Eve, 1934, at the Palm Island Club in Miami. Earl Carroll was bringing his *Vanities* to sunny Florida and Gay was among a dozen starlets on board. Orlova, still a married woman, was seen on the arm of a stockbroker when she arrived in Miami. As fate would have it, Charles "Lucky" Luciano was also scheduled to be in Miami at the time.

On December 28, 1934, Luciano arrived in Miami and, following the rule of law, immediately registered with the police. His information was recorded and they sent him on his way. Lucky was staying at the home of Al Capone's brother Ralph and had plans to see the *Vanities* show on the 31st. That's when Gay Orlova met the scarred, swarthy and well-dressed mobster. "He was lovely to me," she would later recall. And how about the fate of her male companion on this trip? She quickly dismissed him in favor of Lucky's charms. "I even gave up my broker friend just for him."

Charlie was never one to put love before business, but by January of 1935 he and Orlova became quite the item. Back in New York, she moved into his palatial suite at the Waldorff Astoria and the two were full-fledged lovers. Orlova maintained her career, and was still often mentioned by critics and gossip columnists for her beauty and stage presence, but most regularly for her unusual stage name. There were of course detractors. Gay was certainly not the first or last showgirl to usher in sensational fodder for gossip hungry reporters on the hunt for salacious scandal. Many of her colleagues had relationships, or at the very least, were known to mingle in circles with mob types (Marion "Kiki" Roberts with "Legs" Diamond and Evelyn Carmel with George Uffner, for example). Such liaisons gave a bad stereotype to the vocation, and plenty of juicy tidbits for the media and police alike. Individually – both Luciano and Orlova were making quite an impression on society – becoming household names, albeit one for a menacing reputation as a vice lord and the other for sex appeal and choices in male companions.

But as Luciano's status as a high ranking mobster gained more and more notice by law enforcement and the mass media, the love affair would inevitably turn a new corner, one not so welcomed by Gay Orlova. Although it is impossible to know what she really felt for New York's top gangster, Orlova always maintained high praise for Lucky – especially in the press during Thomas E. Dewey's monumental anti-mob crusade against Luciano in 1936.

Lucky decided to high tail it to gangster-friendly Hot Springs Arkansas by mid 1935. The pair remained a couple throughout the period of his 'hiding' in plain sight (although at some point that year, Luciano was rumored to have had an affair with actress Thelma Todd – who died of mysterious circumstances in December). All that came to a halt when Lucky was extradited back to New York in April of 1936. Luciano's legal woes were mounting, so his team of attorneys frantically tried to get good character witnesses, just as Dewey's team was pulling in an army's worth of prosecution witnesses. From a realistic standpoint, Gay Orlova had to have been very aware of Lucky's real career. She was very observant, and as Ed Finn found out the hard way, used it as great tool for manipulation and basic survival throughout her life. But Orlova openly defended Lucky in the press, not to mention the police and prosecutors, without blinking an eye. Columnist Jack Lait once asked her *why* Luciano? She replied, "Oh, I'm infatuated with Lucky. He's so sinister." Notwithstanding her own characterization of Luciano's 'sinister' charm, lawyers wanted her on the stand because they knew the media darling would pack a solid punch of testimony in their client's favor. A few weeks after Lucky was brought back to New York, Orlova railed against the charges brought by Dewey and the scathing media headlines. "Lucky's a perfect gentleman," she insisted. "I don't why they say such mean things about him."

But just as he defiantly claimed having no dealings with any prostitution or white slavery racket (till the day he died), Luciano stood firmly on the decision to not have his lover in court. Lucky told his legal team -"I don't want her mixed up in this case." And so it was... his best witness was out. Thomas E. Dewey however was interested in putting her on the stand for his prosecution case. She was summoned to the offices of Dewey's staff, but Gay Orlova had no intention of offering any information to the prosecution. She strolled in, larger than life, sporting a $4000 fur coat and glimmering jewels. To her dismay, they questioned her about the expensive items. She reportedly couldn't understand how they would consider such items as anything less than basic necessities.

On advice of her friends (plus her own concern over creepy men that seemed to always be following her entourage after Lucky was arrested), Gay Orlova decided to make a quick exit. Lucky didn't want her to testify for him; she absolutely did not want to testify for the prosecution and she didn't want to suffer the same deadly fate that more than a few other witnesses had met. So off the France she went in hopes of avoiding any potential problems attributable to the trial. Charlie "Lucky" Luciano found himself slapped with a 30 to 50 year sentence that summer and was promptly shipped off the to Sing Sing, then Clinton Prison in Dannemora, upstate New York.

In the years following Luciano's incarceration, Orlova found herself in a downward spiral of problems, little of which had anything to do with her former mob boyfriend. Though losing him to the prison system was a severe blow to Orlova (no more life filled with the private planes, custom cars and luxury hotel suites), she continued to bide her time in France while the whole trial and the accompanying danger died down. She planned to return to the States just a year after Lucky was locked down. However, her worst nightmare had just begun to reveal itself.

Immigration officials had commenced proceedings for booting the showgirl out of the country. It was only when she tried to reenter the United States from France in 1937 that she learned the otherwise innocent and naïve young usher groom had the marriage annulled. Headlines like "Uncle Sam Spurns Her" were splashed across newspapers throughout the nation. Gay Orlova, as viewed by officials, was still Galina Orloff and *not* a citizen. She was swiftly deported back to France upon her arrival in New York. Edward Finn later explained he had no idea that his estranged wife was involved with America's most notorious gangster. But when he learned of it – through the media frenzy of the 1936 trial -he made sure the situation would be resolved once and for all. Immigration officials were not about to let Orlova off the hook either. Divorce itself would not have had any effect on Orlova's status in the United States, but annulment changed everything.

She went back to Paris and soon ran into her old flame – the Nobleman (herein lies another mystery – who was this nobleman?). Her situation was still not on solid ground though. Either go back to Russia or stay in France where the government wasn't exactly keen on allowing her to sojourn. The Nobleman and Gay Orlova agreed to a marriage of convenience just three weeks after her arrival in France. She promptly divorced him. Orlova was now a French citizen and felt confident enough to settle in.

Orlova moved quickly to reinvent herself; the blonde coif was transformed back to brunette. In turn, she began a career modeling for clothiers. Still, when she wasn't working, the two former spouses were often seen with each other around the city getting quite cozy. The Broadway rumor mill was always an active gossip playground, so word of Gay's brief marriage reached her counterparts quickly. Many of her old friends back in New York didn't seem to think this marriage was a sham at all.

Then war broke out in Europe and Gay's on again off again relationship with the nobleman took a new turn. He was called to the front lines with the French Army, and she became instantly bored and lonely. While serving along the Maginot border (a fortified span along the border of France and Germany), the nobleman was surprised to see Gay Orlova. She made her way into the war zone somehow, which is a highly unusual accomplishment, especially considering she made no effort to tone down her glitzy style and natural flamboyance. Those qualities, however, soon captured the attention of military police that were also present on the border. There is a fine line between caution and paranoia in wartime. A beautiful, well dressed woman wandering around an abandoned village while military actions are underway was nothing less than a red flag for the other officers. Orlova was quickly taken into to custody by military police. She told her captors she was there to see her husband. Military police then brought the nobleman in for questioning. "She's my fiancée," he told them.

Just those slight inconsistencies, or misspoken details between the two lovers stories was enough to cause the French military to fear espionage. Why else would this woman be here? While in custody, Orlova was told by one of the guards her fate was likely going to be death by firing squad, but that her story was being checked out with officials in Paris. After the infamous tale of Mata Hari… nobody was taking chances with possible spies, and for those suspected - winding up tied to pole for execution had become a very common predicament. Of all the things Gay Orlova may have been – a spy she was not. After six hours of questioning, she was released unharmed and sent back to Paris. The news of Broadway's one-time sweetheart suspected of being a spy and evading the grim reaper spread far and wide, from Europe to the United States. By the fall of 1940 worse rumors floated. The iconic newspaper and radio gossip reporter Walter Winchell (who incidentally was also pivotal in the apprehension of mob boss Louis "Lepke" Buchalter) reported that Orlova was living in near starvation while her French husband was held in a concentration camp. Only a year after that, Winchell's grapevine spewed forth more depressing Orlova rumors. "The ex-Broadway charmer (now wed to a Frenchman) is in Madrid – miserable." Gay Orlova's life had suffering, but never of a dull moment. From living in Manhattan's luxury to nearly being shot in a run down village, and even after the sordid, scandalous and unsatisfying love affairs… she never stopped going after what she wanted.

By 1946, her former gangland lover, Lucky Luciano, had surreptitiously made his way to Cuba. There he would participate in monumental decision-making sessions involving narcotics, gambling and how to handle the financial fiasco of Bugsy Siegel's Flamingo Hotel in Las Vegas. Luciano was a playboy, historically, and besides carrying on casually with various women in his down time, he also had a brief, but publicity ridden, affair with known socialite Beverly Paterno during that period. It seems Lucky's thoughts of Gay Orlova had become fleeting, at best, over the last decade. She, it was rumored in Broadway circles, had thought the two would reunite. Dorothy Kilgallen's *Gossip in Gotham* column summed up much that Orlova probably didn't want to hear. "All those headlines about the reunion Gay Orlova planned with Lucky Luciano came as a complete surprise – not to say shock – to him," she wrote in February of 1946. "He hasn't heard from her in many years."

The last time Gay Orlova's name made the gossip column was in late February of 1948. It was a brief, stark and emotionless passage within a larger piece of entertainment happenings by Walter Winchell. He wrote, *"Lucky Luciano's one-time sweetheart, Gay Orlova (who committed suicide by gas in Paris) apparently became despondent because the wealthy Chilean she expected to marry couldn't get a divorce."* The news of Orlova's fate came in the same week Luciano made headlines for his arrest and deportation by Cuban police.

CHAPTER EIGHT

SELF-INFLICTED WOUNDS

IN THE EARLY morning hours of Sunday July 12th, 1936, a muffled plea for help came across Washington D.C. area phone lines. Hearing the faint desperate request, a quick acting switchboard operator called the police, summoning them to an apartment building located at 1230 New Hampshire Avenue. Responders accustomed to the otherwise shocking images of crimes and injuries were in for a very extraordinary situation when they arrived.

As detectives entered the apartment where the emergency call originated, they observed a female crumpled on the floor. She was bleeding, rambling, naked, and visibly in pain. The smell of natural gas was wafting throughout the living space; police spotted four valves fully opened in the kitchen. The scene looked, at first, very much like an intruder had attempted quite serious harm to this young woman. She was bleeding from flesh wounds to her abdomen and thigh.

The apparent victim was taken to the hospital, where detectives questioned the events of the evening leading to her frantic call for help, while she underwent treatment. She identified herself, at first, by two different names: Margaret Louise Bell and Jean Costello. A third moniker – Jean Bell – was added later. The injured woman then conveyed a tale of stalking and mob torture for the very concerned investigators: At approximately 3:30 in the morning – a man forced his way into her apartment, punched her in the head, bound her hands and feet, and then tore her clothes off before dragging her into the kitchen. She told police that the intruder brandished a sharp object, which he used to carve the letters C and L – four inches high - on her right thigh, and the numbers 3 and 12 on her belly, just beneath her breasts (some reports conversely identified the *initials* as eight inches in diameter and on her abdomen, with the *numbers* carved on her thigh). Bell also stated the man turned on the gas jets and pulled the main phone cord out before he exited her apartment. The detectives were curious how she made the phone call, but Bell explained she had a private phone line installed just a day prior, that the intruder did not see.

The man who committed this violent act, she then told investigators, was one of two mobsters she saw in a nightclub on Saturday evening - and recognized as being associated with Lucky Luciano. How would she know such a thing? She had an answer for that too.

Bell explained that she was among the multitude of witnesses in the Luciano trial, but never had to testify. She assumed, however, that henchmen on Luciano's payroll were looking for revenge because she reneged on an offer to help the gangster's case. She told cops the initials were Luciano's and the numbers signified where those initials were located in the alphabet. At this point, the police believed her nightmarish ordeal was possibly "gangland vengeance." She was vague in specifically identifying her attacker, but told detectives she spotted one or both suspicious men in the nightclub at around 1:00 am.

"It was a fellow named Leo," she said. "He is in the mob. I knew they found me."

Less than a few hours had passed since Bell was discovered and cops were on the hunt for two, possibly three men. Quickly addressing the probability of out of state gangsters, detectives got in touch with two New York investigators, who arrived the following day to assist in what had become more of an interrogation than anything else. Even the office of the man who put Lucky Luciano away – Thomas E. Dewey – was taking the woman's claim seriously.

Bell admitted she had been involved in the white slavery ring (of which Luciano was accused and convicted of heading) since she was sixteen years old, even claimed to have personally met Luciano at one point in time. It was in Cincinnati where she allegedly encountered the gangster in person, but said she knew him only as "a big shot gambler, who won and lost $20,000 in a night," not as the prostitution ring vice lord.

After the prosecution team summoned her in the Luciano trial, Bell said she was held in New York's Women's Detention Center until the Grand Jury would call for her. It was during that time an offer was surreptitiously presented by Luciano associates - for her to speak highly of the mobster's character in a forthcoming news article. The payment was $500. "I didn't want to be unfair to the district attorney," she explained of an uneasy conscious, adding she fled to Washington D.C. just two weeks before the attack.

Detectives found the story a bit peculiar, but not impossible, so they continued to gather her statements. This was an era where vile and inexplicable crimes were common in gangland retribution. Detective Thompson, however, was being very cautious with this woman's story, and soon began an unrelenting line of questioning.

After medical staff patched up Bell's wounds, she was taken to the District of Columbia Women's Bureau. By Monday afternoon a dozen police investigators continued a barrage of fact-finding queries. Bell conferred with her lawyer, but became increasingly nervous, irritated at the endless line of police questions, and her story was developing many holes. By that point, cops learned the twenty-three year old (some sources stated she was twenty-one) went by more aliases than Luciano did; Jean Bell, Jean Arnold and Betty Jaynes among the half dozen fake names. At the precinct, Milton R. Reeves, a bartender who was one of two friends accompanying Bell at the nightclub, was questioned. His version of the earlier events led police to believe he too could identify the perpetrator. However, after several hours with Reeves, police determined something wasn't quite adding up, released him and refused further public comment on it. They also figured out Bell had a history of being a "party girl" and was originally from Lakeland Florida – where she accumulated an even more habitual reputation for manufacturing lurid tales of murder and kidnapping.

Though very suspicious of her story, the police were kept wondering, as Bell did not waver from the basic premise she had been assaulted. News from Baltimore authorities, however, changed the dynamic of Bell's background - they suspected her as the thief of $700 from a war veteran she had been partying with a month prior. She was a tough one to figure out, until she caved, just a little, crying out, "I was only trying to help Charlie!" Chief of Detectives Bernard Thompson was the most skeptical, but publicly stated, "We are investigating this case as an attempted murder."

On July 15, Bell was lined up with several other women and marched before robbery victim Philip R. Davis. He had no reservations in identifying Bell as the red haired woman he spent a night with after an evening of drinking in a Baltimore hotel. Davis said he woke up the next day only to find Bell and his $700 bonus check missing.

The former prostitute, and alleged thief, was just beginning to face the music though. The real test of her horrific incident's merit was coming in the form of another police line up. The mysterious "Leo" she spoke of had been identified as a man that had flown to D.C. the night before the attack, and flew back to New York just hours following the attack. On that information, police apprehended two New York ex-cons and brought them both to Washington D.C. – thirty-six year old Joe Silvers and thirty-four year old Leo Maimone (some media outlets reported his name as *Marmone*), both from Brooklyn. Detailed information on why Silvers was apprehended or his relationship to Bell or Luciano was not made publicly available. Maimone's relation to Lucky Luciano was noted, albeit imprecisely, in news reports as a 'reputed muscle-man' for Luciano's gang (Maimone had made the headlines in 1926 for an attempted armed robbery whereby he was shot in the wrist during a scuffle with police).

If either of the men were responsible for the attempted murder, police expected Bell would be able to pick them out. But this was also a test of her inconsistent story as well. Margaret Louise Bell was going to positively identify her alleged assailants, or was she?

Both men were in the line up of seven total suspects; she could not pick out either of them. Not for lack of trying, Bell told

Detective Thompson "One has a great resemblance, but I can't identify him."

"Which one?" asked Thompson.

"The one with the black and white shirt," she replied.

While it was true that Joe Silvers was wearing such clothing, the detective was thoroughly unconvinced Bell's story had any merit.

After ninety-six hours of near non-stop questioning, paired with her inability to positively identify the attacker, Jean Bell was about to be the subject of criminal charges herself. A U.S. Commissioner released Joe Silvers and Leo Maimone, both of whom pleaded not guilty at arraignment and came prepared with ironclad alibis, from all charges. Bell's story fell completely apart.

"Absolutely groundless," proclaimed Detective Thompson. "A weird fabrication." Margaret Louise Bell crumbled under the pressure, addressing the big question of "Why?" with a negligent reply - "Perhaps I was doped or intoxicated."

Bell's saga of dishonesty dated back to 1931, when she claimed men had shot her in the abdomen. She later admitted the gunshot was self-inflicted. Other incidents included false claims of assault by a black man and having knowledge of multiple unsolved murders in the Sunshine State. Judge C. M. Wiggins of Lakeland Florida had encountered Margaret Louise Bell (and all her alter egos) many times. He noted in a file dating back to her juvenile days -"Margaret has the habit of making up big stories, usually involving herself, which are designed to produce sympathy or notoriety. She makes a pathetic show."

Just a few weeks later, Margaret Louise Bell officially faced larceny charges and was taken into custody by Baltimore police. In a series of events that were never short on odd twists and turns, yet another bombshell - Bell was acquitted of the charges and set free on August 29th. Judge Rowland K. Adams told the courtroom he could certainly come to a conclusion about what really occurred the night Bell and the middle-aged war veteran Philip Davis stayed together, but there wasn't enough solid evidence before him to convict her. The Judge felt the entire truth was not being presented during the trial, probably because of implications that would arise based on the Mann Act (instituted to prohibit white slavery and the interstate transport of females for immoral purposes.) In other words, Judge Adams could probably see that Davis wasn't going to tell the whole story of how and why he was with Bell in the first place, as he too could have found himself in some trouble.

In the end of this mysterious tale, Margaret Louise – aka Jean Bell – walked away from incarceration, but not without scandal that made national headlines. At the root of her salacious story – Charles "Lucky" Luciano – a man that she may or may not have ever actually met. In the wacky world of crime and punishment though, Bell was free and Lucky remained locked away.

CHAPTER NINE

GET OUTTA JAIL CARD

BESIDES THE ORIGINS of his scars and nickname, one of the greatest mysteries of Lucky Luciano's life – *did he really help the Allies win World War II?* A lot of people have read it was true; probably as many or more hoped it was true. Understandably, society would expect a criminal to attempt redemption, and for what better a cause than helping in the war effort. Not that a gangster like Luciano – a man allegedly so vile he was once described as "A shallow parasite" – should be worthy of 'hero' status. But again, helping the good of the nation seems noble and could be viewed as 'welcomed' – for the sake of a greater good.

And then there's the truth. It's a little fuzzy, but contemporary historians and researches have great doubts about just how much Lucky helped the Allied forces. Aren't there lots of stories depicting Luciano as the man who wielded his overlord power, gathering Mafiosi here and abroad to fight the Fascists and Nazis? Yes, there are more than few accounts depicting Lucky Luciano as the driving force behind the invasion of Sicily, and the protection of New York Harbor. Here is another moment in time when the myth overtook the man.

Luciano's conviction for compulsory prostitution in 1936 was, in and of itself, a legal anomaly. Some could and do argue that Special Prosecutor Thomas E. Dewey was merely a politically motivated egomaniac dead set on taking down an equally narcissistic kingpin by any means necessary. Other could and do argue that like in the case of Al Capone – this is a recognized, hands down, undeniable bad guy in general, so *how* you get him isn't as important as just making sure you get him.

Ronald Fino, author of *The Triangle Exit* and former FBI operative, knows it's not unusual to use whatever resources are available to get the bad guys. "*I think it was convenient,*" Fino says *of the Luciano case. "And they wanted to get him."*

Realistically, and even though Luciano denied it until the day he died, the top mob guys would have probably been making some money from even the lowest level rackets – including prostitution, for which he was convicted. They were insulated of course, and Luciano possibly had not any near the involvement with the madams, bookers or pimps the prosecution accused him of. However skewed or questionable the prosecution's tactics were – reputation truly doomed Lucky Luciano.

Things were about to change for him after a suspicious case of intentional or accidental damage occurred to a retrofitted troop ship in New York harbor. Docked at the 48th pier, on February 9, 1942, the French ocean liner *Normandie* (renamed the U.S.S. Lafayette) catches fire and capsizes on its side.

Naval officials began suspecting sabotage, and for good reason. Even before the United States entered in to World War II – the government knew that Nazi subs were trolling up and down the

East Coast, and there was the American Nazi Party or Bund as it was called.

Fear and paranoia overshadowed practicality though, as often happens during conflicts of any kind. So it happened, a month after the ship was damaged, Commander Charles Radcliffe Haffenden, Office of Naval Intelligence approached New York's Assistant District Attorney – Murray Gurfein – to discuss the possibility of employing underworld denizens for protection. To be fair, the mob was certainly know for successful "protection rackets" and everyone in New York knew who really controlled the docks.

It wasn't long before Luciano's attorney, Moses Polakoff, rounded up Meyer Lansky and Frank Costello to discuss the possibility of helping out the cause. According to some sources, and a lot of gangland lore, Lansky and Bugsy Siegel were among a throng of Jewish gangsters quite fond of busting up Bund meetings on their free time. Lansky was also known as vocally very patriotic. It is said Bugsy once attended a party in Europe where two prominent Nazis, Goebbels and Goering, were also in attendance; he was talked out of killing them on the spot by his date – Countess di Frasso.

In February of 1943, Judge McCook heard attorney Polakoff's request for Luciano's appeal. It was denied, but the Judge makes note of Luciano's assistance to the Office of Naval Intelligence. Throughout this time, Lucky had been transferred from the cold and dank Clinton Prison to Great Meadow Correctional Facility– where mob buddies meet him on several more occasions.

Allegedly, Luciano also used his pull to recruit Sicilian mafia to assist the Allied Invasion. Author Tim Newark, in the book *The Mafia At War*, noted whereby Meyer Lansky recalled how gangster Joe Adonis would throw Lucky's name around to Sicilians, in order to get their cooperation in the war effort:

"Sometimes some of the Sicilians were very nervous. Joe would just mention the name of Lucky Luciano and say he had given them orders to talk. If the Sicilians were still reluctant, Joe would stop smiling and say, 'Lucky will not be pleased to hear that you have not been helpful.'"

Now, did Lucky really provide secret assistance to the Office of Naval Intelligence? And, did he have mobsters in New York secure the docks from further sabotage?

To the latter question, *Normandie's* damage was likely the result of an electrical fire – not Nazi sabotage (and not mob sabotage, which was also a tall tale). And the former... well, Haffendon came under scrutiny by his own office after making recommendations on behalf of Lucky's supposed help. Haffendon denied every requesting Luciano actually be paroled, but there were many questions raised regarding the help of New York's underworld.

Still, whatever Lucky Luciano did or didn't do for the war effort, he was headed for freedom – sort of. The very man who put Luciano away on a 30 to 50 year sentence – Thomas E. Dewey – was now Governor of New York, and he was letting Lucky off the hook.

The Governor's office announced on January 3, 1946 that Luciano's sentence was being commuted. The event made headlines the following day. Dewey, however, made sure to also denounce Luciano's past by recounting all the white slavery and racketeering he was guilty of, just as a reminder he did the right thing back in 1936 and nobody should forget what kind of guy Lucky was. But then Dewey explained why he signed the commutation order:

"Upon the entry of the United States into the war, Luciano's aid was sought by the armed forces in inducing others to provide information concerning possible enemy attack. It appears that he co-operated in such effort, though the actual value of the information procured is not clear."

Whatever actually happened, to convince Dewey to commute the sentence, must have been of some merit, or importance. Historian and publisher of organized crime history journal, *Informer*, Thomas Hunt says there's just not a lot of solid evidence for Lucky being a war hero.

"I don't believe Lucania personally made any positive contribution to the allied war effort," Hunt says. "But I am fairly well convinced that anti-Fascist elements in the Sicilian underworld did assist American forces to a degree. I simply haven't seen any evidence of a meaningful link between Lucania and the Sicilian Mafia while the war was raging in Europe and he was held in prison in New York.

Dewey took heat for years over the decision. Haffendon was forced to transfer (he was also faulted for often commiserating and playing golf with Frank Costello). The repercussions for letting Luciano off the hook didn't seem all that worth it. Either Luciano really did make the docks safe and invasion into Sicily possible, or... something else.

"You know how I got out?" Luciano rhetorically asked reporter Oscar Fralfy. "This is the truth. I told my lawyers to get together everything they could on a certain man. They had a book full of stuff. Then my lawyer walked in, threw it on his desk, and told him if I wasn't deported, anything to get out of prison, this would made pubic information."

The most logical "man" one might consider was the target of Luciano's wrath – Thomas E. Dewey. But Charlie never named anyone specifically, just intimated it was someone of presumed "good standing" in society and or politics.

"They think I was bad," Lucky continued. "They should have seen what we had on him, this honorable public servant."

Another theory however comes from author Darwin Porter's 2012 book *J. Edgar Hoover & Clyde Tolson: Investigating the Sexual Secrets of America's Most Famous Men and Women*. Porter points to rumors that FBI boss Hoover – who notably denied the existence of the Mafia for many years – was often given "sure bets" at the track by Frank Costello, who was of course in collusion with bookie Frank Erickson. According to this theory, Hoover (known also for keeping files on anyone and everyone) was himself the subject of a figurative "file" kept by guys Porter calls *"The Unholy Three"* - Meyer Lansky, Lucky Luciano and Frank Costello. This theory, accurate or not, does manage to throw another monkey wrench into the whole "How did Lucky get out of jail" conundrum. The FBI, in fact, stated in 1946 the department saw no substantial assistance from Luciano in the war effort. Hoover himself had written a report on Haffendon, which read:

"A shocking example of misuse of Navy authority in interest of a hoodlum. It surprises me they didn't award Luciano the Navy Cross."

Conflicting theories and untold instances of secrecy make this a great mystery in both Luciano's tale and that of American history overall. What is a fact though? Lucky Luciano was placed on a ship set for Palermo Sicily, on February 8th, 1946. He was officially a free man, under the stipulation he was never to return to the United States again.

CHAPTER TEN

GANGSTER'S PARADISE

THE SEEMINGLY ENDLESS supply of cash potential present in the Caribbean was impossible to resist. Criminal overlords from New York to Chicago to New Orleans and beyond were gnawing at the bit for a piece of the giant gambling pie by the late 1930's. Mobsters among them included Meyer Lansky, Frank Costello from New York, Al Capone's *Outfit* men from Chicago, and Santo Trafficante's Florida operation. First it was Miami and the "carpet joints" (slang term for luxury casino) they took over. Gambling was, as these men saw it a decade before, going to replace liquor rackets. They knew prohibition on alcohol would not last forever, so like any forward thinking corporation – they examined risk and reward of other enterprises.

From the sand and sun of South Florida to the island paradise of Cuba, they wanted locations oozing with easily bought politicians. Corruption at the highest levels is and always was the main ingredient for organized crime to flourish. Havana was beautiful. The Royal Cuban palms lined the streets; extravagant hotels drew celebrities and high rollers alike. And... the heads of state were, in many cases, enticed by the enormous amounts of tax-free cash the gangsters from America were promising.

Lucky Luciano was kept in the loop of all the Syndicate dealings, while he awaited release from prison. He most likely anticipated a quick move to Cuba, after his release, to fully immerse himself in the lucrative and growing gambling business, and be closer to the United States. However, that plan was of course not as easily carried out, as he was – under condition of release – immediately exiled to Italy. And... not permitted in the United States again. Luciano wanted to be in America, perhaps more than anything else he ever craved. Cuba would have to do for the time being, but that too would take some 'working' of the system.

Stories of how Luciano made the journey from Italy to Cuba are varied. The media and some law enforcement investigations showed he used the name Lucania on paperwork to travel first to South America, then on to Cuba. He arrived in October 1946, taking up a room in one of the lavish hotels. Within months, he lived in a luxurious home in the exclusive area of Miramar. He was quite settled in with no intentions of leaving.

However, he was being noticed. His presence was attracting unwanted attention, for the gangster himself and Cuban officials who assisted his entrance into the country. First, the December conference held at the Hotel Nacional in Havana. Sometimes referred to as the *Havana Mob Convention*, it was a weeklong event filled with business and pleasure. Gangsters from all over the continental United States made their way to the island for the monumental meeting. Also present... entertainer Frank Sinatra. Stories about the context of such a meeting include the decision to murder Benjamin "Bugsy" Siegel, narcotics trafficking, and of course the mainstay of the mob's Cuban interests – gambling.

Rumors and theories about this 'convention' have circulated and been interpreted in various ways. But, there are some notable truths to the story, all of which led to Luciano's eventual deportation from the island paradise. First, Luciano had begun an affair with a known socialite named Beverley Paterno. She enjoyed the limelight, and publicity that comes with it. To Luciano's dismay… Cuban press had taken photos of the pair on several occasions.

The final nail in the coffin, however, was the presence of a young, cocky and ambitious reporter named Robert Ruark. He happened to be in Havana at the same time as the mob convention – and he realized quickly what a goldmine of media goodies he stumbled onto. He saw Luciano and Sinatra cavorting with party girls and gangsters alike. Ruark was in his glory; both Luciano and Sinatra would be the basis of colorfully written vengeance in his columns for years.

"He (Sinatra) was here for four days last week," Ruark wrote in an article titled *Sinatra Sets Poor Example for Followers*, "His companion in public and private was Luciano, Luciano's bodyguards, and a rich collection of gamblers and highbinders."

Ruark made further light of the criminal and celebrity grandeur, adding – "In addition to Mr. Luciano, I am told that Ralph Capone was present. This I cannot prove, since I wasn't invited to the party myself. But Mr. Luciano was definitely there, and so was a rather large and well-matched assortment of the goons who find the South salubrious in the winter, or grand-jury time. The party, liberally spangled with young and pretty girls, was hurled, I am told by Jorge Sanchez, a big sugar fellow."

United States officials took Ruark's observations very seriously. One agent in particular was hell bent on bringing Luciano down – Harry J. Anslinger. He was the Commissioner of the

Federal Bureau of Narcotics. Before that – Prohibition Commissioner. Anslinger, untill his death in 1975, battled on the front lines of the drug wars. It can be said with a great deal of accuracy – Anslinger hated drugs and truly believed in what he was doing. For Luciano, this was bad news. Anslinger had it out for Lucky, convinced heroin and cocaine was pouring into the U. S. since the gangster moved to Cuba.

Anslinger was not happy with how he perceived Cuba's lackadaisical effort to thwart dope trafficking in the past. "We told Cubans exactly who was responsible for the acts at their end of the situation, "he said of an incident a year prior. "But not one arrest was ever made. This time we decided to take action on our own first."

That action he took was the immediate stoppage of all legal medical narcotic shipments to the island. Anslinger wanted Luciano deported back to Italy. The pressure on Cuban officials was heavy. They really feared Anslinger wasn't bluffing, so a move was made by Cuban Secret Police to apprehend and deport Luciano so as not to disrupt the flow of medicine any longer than necessary.

On February 22, 1947, Luciano is arrested in a café. Secret Police escorted him to the immigration bureau where he is detained and questioned. Anslinger showed no signs of patience, insisting the embargo on medicine would continue until Luciano was in Italy. Five days later, Cuba's President decreed Luciano an "Undesirable Alien in Cuba," in a bold move to ease tensions with the United States. Ironically, the U.S. Embassy informed Cuban officials that no embargo was ever actually placed on shipments of medicine! Despite the obvious and offensive scare tactics made by Anslinger, by March – Luciano was indeed deported, placed on a Turkish freighter headed back to mainland Italy.

Lucky Luciano was certainly not the only one losing a mob hot spot. By 1953, a revolution was hatched. Led by Fidel Castro and Ernesto "Che" Guevara, it would not only bring about total political change, but also oust the mobsters and all their lucrative gambling empires. 1959 was truly the end of the 'Gangster's Paradise.'

CHAPTER ELEVEN

A LEGEND IN HIS OWN CRIME

"Every time some two-cent bum gets arrested, they say he was a pal of mine, and when some other two-cent bum get killed, they say I ordered him killed. Somebody I don't know from Adam."

Charles "Lucky" Luciano to columnist Earl Wilson, 1949

THE 1950'S DIDN'T have a jazzed up name like the *Roaring Twenties*, but is often referred to as *The Golden Years*, or *Golden Era*. Even though the "Cold War" was rearing its ugly head for the first time, the period from 1950 to 59 was, for the most part, a positive period of technology and prosperity in the United States.

The era was also a special time for Lucky Luciano, although not without pivotally vexing and somber moments. He was confined to Italy, and granted he didn't like that much, but he was in love like never before, and perhaps most interesting – he was mellowing out. Decades of negative press, years of police scrutiny, and a lifetime of secrets kept, but now he was beginning to air out things that haunted him. No, not everything! Charlie was a lifetime mobster that rarely gave up all the "goods" on anyone or anything. Still, he was at a point in his life where granting some interviews, expressing some regrets, and clearing his name a little went hand in hand with the simple joys, such as spending his days with girlfriend Igea Lissoni, his dogs, espresso in a café, and a strong desire to talk with anyone from America! He had even claimed to be free from indulging in cigarettes and the very vice he made a fortune from – booze.

Luciano's legendary life was again capturing the attention of the public. He was considering movie pitches made by would-be producers, treating journalists to breakfast, and even talking to authorities with less reservation. However, Lucky still had a sharp tone threaded through his dialogue when it came to thoughts on law enforcement. Underhanded compliments powered by a lingering jadedness spilled out from time to time.

"If I was starting all over again," Luciano once told Alfred Klein, former Associate Counsel of the Senate Crime Investigating Committee, "That's what I'd be, lawyer, doctor or cop. You'll find some cops are honest; it's a shame more of them aren't. But there are many who look on their badge as a license to steal."

His arch nemesis in the 1940's was inarguably Harry J. Anslinger, but the 1950's introduced him to a new foe – Charles Siragusa. A Federal Narcotics agent, Siragusa made Charles Luciano his lifelong target (Anslinger was fully behind him), beginning in 1951 when he testified before a Senate committee, condemning soft rules on drug traffickers' ability to gain visas. Standing before the committee members, Siragusa also proclaimed Luciano, "The Kingpin" of dope in Italy and the United States. The agent had moved to Italy, spent much of his time tracking down drug smugglers and their bases of operations throughout Europe and parts of the Middle East. He believed, fully, that most of the narcotics entering the United States somehow had Luciano's figurative prints all over it. There wasn't any hard evidence found, in the years Siragusa dogged Luciano, most of it was circumstantial (and the two only met face to face once, accidentally, in a restaurant). Still, the agent was a big thorn in Luciano's side for over a decade.

The debate over how much or how little Luciano was actually involved in narco trafficking still endures. Thomas Hunt, publisher of the organized crime history quarterly *The Informer Journal,* isn't entirely convinced Lucky was a drug kingpin, but notes the possibility existed.

"It is difficult to imagine Lucania personally controlling the worldwide flow of heroin while his activities and communications were closely watched by Italian police and agents of the U.S. Bureau of Narcotics," Hunt explains. "But something must have been at the root of official suspicions."

Lucky's most outspoken advocate during all the legal aggravations was Igea Lissoni. They met in the late 1940's, but by the time their friendship turned romantic – Lissoni's family disowned her. They, apparently, could not tolerate their daughter – a former and well-known ballerina from Milan – commiserating with the infamous gangster.

News briefs would, from time to time, announce that Lucky and Igea were married. Luciano always maintained the pair was never legally married. Igea was, if anyone ever could be, Luciano's one true love, but most of the marriage talks originated in popular gossip columns. There were also rumors suggesting he still had affairs or mistresses on the side, but in reality it seemed most of his time was spent with Igea.

A New York writer named Llewellyn Miller visited Lucky and Igea in Naples, fall of 1952. She was one of a handful of eager reporters Luciano had granted interviews over the golden era period. In the presence of a burly Luciano bodyguard named Benny Dusso, Igea Lissoni and Lucky himself, Miller was able to paint a vivid picture of the then fifty-five year old gangster. "His manner is markedly quiet. There is an air of watchful restraint about him," she noted of his demeanor. Physically though, she described his features as well kept, small hands and feet, beautifully cut suit and conservative tie. "The famous drooping eyelid," she concluded, "must have been fixed by a plastic surgeon because both eyes open now to the same extent."

As the decade unfolded, so too did Luciano's eagerness to have his version of events told in a film or book. Most accounts of a book or movie deal stems from the 1960's meetings with producer Martin Gosch (and the controversial 1975 publication of "The Last Testament of Lucky Luciano."). However, Lucky entertained offers for his life story before Gosch came into the picture. The first newsmaker was actually independent producer Phil Tucker. Known primarily for short segment television productions and the cult sci-fi film *Robot Monster* (1953) Tucker's name quickly became a target for ridicule, especially from Luciano's old foe Robert Ruark. The unapologetic columnist must've been so giddy with scandalous joy at the news, he didn't even get Tucker's first name correct!

"The chances are awful good that a Hollywood producer named Bill Tucker won't get very far with a projected film on the life and hard times of Mr. Charles Lucky Luciano," Ruark wrote in a piece titled *Deodorizing Luciano Doomed to Fail*. Further into the lambasting commentary, Ruark added, "I don't know this Tucker, who supposed to do the documentary on poor old Charlie Lucky, but if he's looking to make a sociological accident out of a Sicilian hoodlum – he's looking for a lump."

Ironically, Ruark's prediction was sort of correct. Tucker was offered some $300,000 from Luciano's faction to produce the film – with conditions. At first, Tucker seemed fine with Lucky having final say on the finished product, but the deal collapsed a month later. No Hollywood studio wanted to touch it, probably because of the mob tie rumors swarming around the source of funding. In November of '52, Tucker announced the project officially dead. "I thought maybe I could film it my way and tell the truth," Tucker explained. "But Luciano insisted on showing he was framed and this I couldn't do."

The following year, far more pressing issues arose. Igea Lissoni began having health issues. Lucky made an attempt to get her treatment in the United States. A failed attempt, but a gossip column took note of her visa being denied. Lissoni had developed breast cancer; another attempt to get her into the States was made in late 1954. It too was in vain. She and Luciano continued to make the best of their situation – legal, medical and otherwise – remaining together as a couple until 1958.

Igea Lissoni, just thirty-seven years old, lost her battle with cancer in late 1958. Charles Luciano was, his friends often told the media, absolutely beside himself with grief. For two years after her death, he wore a black tie and armband in mourning. Some said he was never the same after Igea died. If anything, it made him really want to leave some sort of legacy for the world (he had become even more intent on telling his story in film or book form). News reports here and there claimed he had a new mistress, a young woman named Rita Motolo, within a year of Lissoni's passing, but Charlie sternly denied the affair. As for the marriage mystery, Luciano explained to reporter Jack Anderson in 1959, "The life I was living, I knew that one day I was going to finish up in jail or with a bullet in me. I didn't think it was right to take a wife and have kids."

CHAPTER TWELVE

POSTHUMOUS REAPPEARANCE

FINAL HOURS

On January 26, 1962, movie producer Martin Gosch arrived at the Capodichino Airport in Naples, Italy. The purpose of his visit – another meeting with Charles "Lucky" Luciano, information gathering for the purported film project. Luciano had been questioned by police earlier in the day, this time about a multi-national smuggling ring. He was tired, and it was showing in his face. But Luciano arrived to greet Gosch at the airport, looking elegantly adorned in blue jacket and gray slacks, ready to discuss the project in more detail. With Lucky was an English-speaking officer named Cesare Resta. As Gosch and Luciano chatted, they indulged in some fruit juice at the bar, before making their way out to a vehicle. The trio never made it to Luciano's car. Just outside the terminal the infamous gangster was heard to say, "Martin, Martin…" then collapsed to the floor. It was just after 5 pm.

Luciano died that day, but the mysteries and conspiracies were far from over. In fact, rumors began almost immediately. Two days later, a preliminary autopsy found the cause of death most likely a heart attack. However, on February 9th, Italian newspaper, *Telesara,* announced an autopsy report showed Luciano was poisoned by potassium cyanide. The paper claimed a medical examination found traces of the poison in the viscera (abdominal and thoracic areas). The newspaper, running with rumors that began in Naples when Luciano was again under suspicion for narcotics activities, suggested Luciano was murdered, or it was suicide to avoid prosecution. Authorities in the United States were far more cautious in taking the news report too seriously that early on in the investigation.

Italian investigators concurred. "The experts' appraisal is not yet complete," warned an Italian state prosecutor, "Therefore, one cannot speak of poisoning."

A Grand Send Off

Luciano had longed for a return to the United States. In death, his family tried very hard to gain approval for the remains to be transported to New York. In the meantime, his brother Bartolo and nephew Salvatore travelled to Italy for a grand funeral service.

On Monday, January 29th, 1962 – Salvatore Lucania was laid to rest, temporarily, in Naples. Luciano's body was transported in an elegant hearse, drawn by eight horses. The service included a Requiem Mass and was attended by hundreds of mourners, family and of course law enforcement officials from both the United States and Italy – equipped with cameras. There was also much fanfare. One woman, of whom a newspaper described as "a Neapolitan beauty" said she was Luciano's widow. A headline in the Sydney Morning Herald read, *"Slums Mourn Lucky"* Lu-

ciano," and went on to report how the poor loved Lucky's visits and generosity.

There were many individuals in attendance that authorities wanted to keep tabs on. Most of these men tried to conceal their faces from the press and police cameras, but to little avail.

"You can't tell them without a scorecard, "said a police official of the numerous underworld mourners present. "But I'm sure that when the films are developed they come in very useful, if not now, in the future."

As for the 'mystery' woman claiming to be the wife of Luciano, well, nothing much of detail was immediately reported. However, five months after Luciano's funeral service in Naples, *Parade Magazine* reported a story by Jack Anderson that suggested, demonstrated really, Luciano had one final mistress before his death. The article described the woman as "young" and "pigeon-plump." Her name was Adriana Rizzo; personal photos of she and Lucky accompanied the article. (Rizzo was also found to be, in 1974, one of five recipients of royalties from the highly controversial book *The Last Testament of Lucky Luciano* that Gosch and Richard Hammer co-authored).

Going Home

The myth-busting truth behind Lucky's death was not fully divulged until June, when Italian authorities wholeheartedly denounced the poisoning theory, stating Luciano definitively died of a heart attack. By that time, Luciano's wish of going home to America had come true. His body was taken to St. Johns Cemetery, Queens New York, in February. He was interred in a $30,000 vault, adorned with a stained glass crypt window depicting a Saint. Someone allegedly asked Lucky's brother, Bartolo, which saint it was, to which he replied, "I don't know. I don't have much to do with saints."

Bogus Reporting

Back to the poisoning rumor, and how it got started in the first place. There were plenty of onlookers present when Luciano fell to the ground, clutching the arm of Martin Gosch. Inaccurate speculation reared its ugly head, most likely, when some of these bystanders witnessed Gosch placing something in Luciano's mouth. And again, in Naples there had been chatter about Luciano being in trouble with police and/or drug lords. How quickly an event snowballs into conspiracy. Gosch was even mistakenly reported as being a "visiting Spaniard" – which also played right into the hand of gossip because Luciano had been under scrutiny for a "Spanish" link in a smuggling operation. The truth is… Gosch was very aware of Luciano's heart problems and was trying to save the man's life with the medication.

Book Backlash

Martin Gosch had, over the couple years he kept in contact with Luciano, faced a few obstacles in his plans for a film of Lucky's life. Luciano had visitors and letters that were said to be warnings. Some of his old cronies back home weren't too keen on a movie depiction of mob life. Luciano allegedly gave in to the firm requests and offered Gosch an alternative – write a book but not publish until ten years after his death. Furthermore, it was not Gosch that even originated the idea of a film. A man named Charles Duke, allegedly, was an old associated of Luciano and pitched the film idea directly. When Lucky agreed, Duke brought Gosch on board to write the script and produce a film version.

Gosch never recorded any of the conversations with Luciano; always handwritten notes. This decision on Gosch's part would lead to much skepticism when the book, *The Last Testament of Lucky Luciano*, was released in 1975. Gosch died in 1973, and his wife allegedly disposed of all his records and notes. Richard Hammer, whom Gosch joined forces with to co-author the book, worked with what material he had. Before the book was released, it came under heavy fire for inconsistencies. Detractors didn't believe the words were actually Luciano's – at least not all of them – and many recollections in the book did not match up with known facts.

Richard Hammer, in several post publication interviews, maintained the bulk of the book was how Luciano told it. He admitted some creative license in how dialogue was written, but that it was, even if embellished by Luciano, still the gangster's own words.

Another related twist to the Gosch element was the proposed actor set to play Luciano in the film version. Actor Cameron Mitchell had been issued death threats after he signed on to play the part – a week before Luciano died.

"I haven't decided not to play the part of Luciano after receiving these letters," Mitchell told the press. "You see, I am bound by a contract I signed with American producer Martin Gosch." Mitchell also remarked how "very upset" he was at the three insidious letters written in "very bad English."

Mitchell's safety was again threatened in December 1962, almost a year after Luciano had died. Perpetrators, alleged to be from the American mafia, had issued warnings that if he even 'translated' for a film version of a Luciano biopic – he young son, Cameron Jr., would be kidnapped. This was the first recorded incident of a direct kidnapping threat against an American actor.

As it turned out though, Gosch never made that movie after all (though a film was produced by others, starring Rod Steiger and appearance by drug agent Charles Siragusa in 1973.)

Angry Much?

Narcotics Agent Charles Siragusa, Lucky's archrival in the 1950's, was cast as himself in a film version of the Luciano story that was released in 1973. But Siragusa was still fuming over not getting his man. Of Luciano's death in 1962, Siragusa remarked, "I was angry because my office was on the verge of making a conspiracy case against him and I felt it wasn't decent of him to die."

And that's not all Siragusa had to say about Lucky Luciano. In a time when there was no such thing as political correctness – Siragusa bluntly, offensively, let loose: "When a man is young he dreams of being in bed with the most beautiful woman in the world, but me – and I'm no queer – I dreamed of pinching Luciano."

A Warden's Recollection

In 1981, former prison guard and Warden Donald Byington gave an interview to reporters that shed some interesting light on a few infamous gangsters. Byington had, at one time or another in his care, the likes of Legs Diamond, Louis Lepke, Al Capone and Lucky Luciano.

Of Capone, Byington said he was "a big, fat slob," who was constantly in fear for his life. "If I had to pick the most dangerous person," the retired Warden recalled, "It was Luciano."

Terror in the 2000's

In a little known incident – one of the most bizarre claims to arise - Lucky Luciano's name was brought up after the September 11, 2001 terror attacks. A married couple, both of whom were scientific researchers, met with FBI agents in California on September 24, 2001 – to share information regarding 'financing' they claimed to be knowledgeable of, concerning the terror attacks. The FBI interviewed the pair, listening to a story of Vatican financing and mob affiliation behind the perpetrators of the September 11th attacks.

In a 2004 memorandum, FBI agents stated of the woman's claims, "Then told the agents that she was adopted, but had recently discovered the identity of her true father. Her father was Salvatore "Lucky" Luciano, noted Mafioso, and her mother was a woman who was related to the individuals who control the Vatican's finances and the Vatican Bank."

After a thorough investigation of the terror-related claims – the FBI concluded there was no substance to any of the tales.

"It is recommended that no additional investigation be conducted into the claims."

Pop Culture Nonpareil

"Modern popular culture transmitted via mass media and aimed particularly at younger people." – Oxford Dictionary

"The types of entertainment that most people in a society enjoy, for example movies, television programs, and popular music" – Macmillan Dictionary

"Music, TV, cinema, literature, etc. that is popular and enjoyed by ordinary people, rather than experts or very educated people" – Cambridge Dictionary

Fifty years after his death and Charles "Lucky" Luciano is still a great subject of discussion. While not everyone in America is familiar with his history, a lot will recognized the name, if for nothing more than that name has been embedded in popular culture. So, why then? What is it about Luciano that sells shirts, posters, magazines, comics, newspapers, movies and... yes, just like this one you're reading... books?

"Good or bad," explains David Brooks, owner of mob themed t-shirt company The American Gangsters, "there are always going to be fans of Lucky. He may not be a household name like Al Pacino, Derek Jeter or even Spider man but he has fans. With younger kids learning about the mafia in high school and Hollywood making movies and TV shows about the mob. There are museums all across the country that are dedicated to the mob."

For organized crime researchers and historians, Luciano is a wonderful topic because, as hopefully this book demonstrates, there's a seemingly endless supply of conjecture and vintage reports to sift through. It's frustrating, alluring and fun – trying to discover how one individual – a criminal – could affect so much of society and economics.

"Early on, readers were interested in the sensationalized accounts of his underworld career," says Thomas Hunt, Publisher of *Informal Journal*. "These days, they appear to be interested in reading about the facts behind the earlier myths. Unfortunately, the out-of-date information still influences many minds and causes the continued growth of legends that already have been disproven."

And of course, there has always been an American love affair with gangland tales in general. Luciano, Capone, Gotti, Barnes, Blanco, and Escobar are some of real life fascinations, and of course the reel life examples *Goodfellas, The Godfather, and American Gangster*. The romantic notion of organized crime, all too often, overtakes the reality.

"I believe that the names of Lucky Luciano, Al Capone, John Gotti and other criminal kingpins are prevalent because of the glamour that is attributed to their lifestyles by the media, coupled with a sense of curiosity on the part of average Americans who view them as being so different from them. Most people are inclined to follow the rules and they are intrigued by those who 'make their own rules,' explains ATF Agent Pete Forcelli.

Ronald Fino, author and former FBI operative agrees. "Throughout history the public has always had a fascination with criminals such as Jesse James –Billy the Kid – John Dillinger, etc. The same holds true for the mafia. The public sees these thugs as successful, killing only those that have greedily ventured into their wraith and probably deserved killing. What they do not know, or close their eyes to the widespread damage they cause to those who admire them such as stock fraud, illegal dumping of hazardous waste, pension fund theft etc. Police are unfortunately viewed as bullies and will do anything to put mobsters behind jail."

Beside the law-abiding segment of society, without question – individuals like Luciano are often looked upon with a more sinister worldview and admiration. Forcelli adds, "In New York, most citizens have forgotten Lucky Luciano. The exception is those who have chosen to follow a life of crime. To those people, Luciano is a role model. His reputation for installing fear in the community is coveted and sometimes emulated. It wasn't uncommon to find posters of Luciano in the homes of hardcore criminals during search and arrest warrants. They were commonly found with posters from the movie "Scarface" in drug dealer's homes. The obvious difference being that Pacino was playing a fictional character. Luciano was real."

Seth Ferranti, incarcerated author of *The Supreme Team* and *Rayful Edmond: Washington D.C.'s Most Notorious Drug Lord*, says even in prison – people still look up to Luciano.

"High profile gangsters are still held in awe by the prisoner population and guards alike. It is just a part of American culture; we are obsessed with fame even in prison. That is just how it goes."

Mob movies, fictional and those based on true stories, are big business at the box office. If a film is good, or at the very least has strong marketing – fans will flock. As recently as 2007, Hollywood reports divulged information concerning another Luciano movie. In 2013, there were indications of two different Luciano themed films in the works; one based on *The Last Testament of Lucky Luciano*, and the other drawn from the recollections of a former Luciano bodyguard. (IMDB has an entry for one of these films, scheduled to release in 2014).

We may never be able to fully comprehend how certain figures, over others, become ingrained in popular culture. What is known… money to be made from the marketing of such things seems endless. It's not all that different, when you really think about it, from what was going on with the gangster's mindset for business opportunities. Regardless of ethical implications… if there's a demand – there will be suppliers!

CHAPTER THIRTEEN

IT'S A RAP!

Rap Sheet: Slang for *Record of Arrest & Prosecution*

FOR ALL INTENT and purpose, it is fair to say Charlie was a 'career' criminal. Or, as author Gerald Posner says, "The myth became bigger than the man, and that gave him even more street cred." His police record dated back to the teenage years and continued through 1936. It should be noted that Luciano arrested was several times (mostly in Italy) after his 1936 incarceration, but usually for suspicion and little solid evidence. However, until his death in 1962, he was always under surveillance and scrutiny by law enforcement, and the press, both nationally and internationally. Such is the existence for a known organized crime leader – forever looking over one's shoulder.

With regard to his illicit exploits and punishment thereof, again to reiterate, Luciano is most recognized for the headline making 1936 "Compulsory Prostitution" case that earned him a thirty to fifty year sentence. However, his law-breaking trajectory started at a young age and lasted for half a century (if he was indeed still calling the shots in his later years), guided by an unwavering desire for wealth and power based on illicit goods and services. The prostitution charge was a dramatic exploit that made prosecutors and politicians famous, while putting names like Luciano on the national map of public recognition. Although more than a few of the incidents surrounding Luciano's legend seem to have taken on a life of their own – the prostitution case trumped everything, making it one of the most media frenzied criminal trials ever covered.

We may never positively know some of the answers or details lurking behind every infraction, yet we can always examine the recorded history of Charles "Lucky" Luciano's rap sheet to further discuss and debate the possibilities. Some underworld figures are, for better or worse, always interesting subject matter for discourse. Here is the crime chronology – a few of the more interesting entries are given special attention and detail. Also of note... Luciano was 'suspected' of involvement in several crimes for which he was never actually arrested for, among those being the murders of Masseria, Maranzano and Dutch Schultz.

6/26/1916

Violation Section 246, a narcotics violation. While working for a hat company, Luciano is caught selling heroin, which is conveniently hidden in a hatbox, delivered to a prostitute (working as a police informer). He is convicted for the crime, but released on parole in December of that year. This was the first factual account of Luciano's interest in illicit drugs.

12/22/1921

Criminally carrying a weapon. His luck was truly beginning to kick in, with regard to getting off the hook. The charges were quickly dismissed.

8/28/1922

Business code violation. This is the first of his "Violation of Corporation Ordinance" arrests (basically, traffic citations and similar infractions). He was fined five dollars. He accumulates ten more of such violations from 1922 to 1926. **One notable exception is on July 27 – Luciano and Joe Scalise are pulled over for running a stop light; police find a shotgun and two handguns in the car. Thomas E. Dewey would later use Luciano's response – as to *why they had weapons* - against him in the 1936 Compulsory Prostitution trial to further make the gangster look like a common uneducated hoodlum. The exchange of dialogue allegedly went like this:

Officer: "What were you hunting?"

Luciano: "Oh, peasants."

Officer: "Pheasants?"

Luciano: "Yeah, that's right. Pheasants."

The charge was dismissed.

6/2/1923

Harrison Act Violation. Luciano is arrested after peddling two ounces of pure heroin to an informant for the U.S. Secret Service. Days later, he again sells the drug to the same informant (one ounce). He is charged by FBN (Federal Bureau of Narcotics – the predecessor to the DEA), but Luciano agrees to direct authorities to a stash house where they would find a larger quantity of heroin – 163 Mulberry Street, Manhattan. He is spared prosecution for his cooperation.

12/29/1926

Felonious Assault. A car of four gunmen fired shots at Albert Levy, an insurance broker, and his chauffeur on December 21st.

Levy is hospitalized from wounds to arms and wrist, and informs police he knows who committed the assault. Luciano, Legs Diamond, Ed Diamond and Fatty Walsh are arrested by a team of twenty police officers in connection to the robbery attempt. However, Levy has a change of heart after two of the suspects are paraded before him in the hospital room, and tells police, "There's some mistake. These aren't the men." All four are discharged.

7/6/1927

Disorderly Conduct. Specifically, this was a gambling charge. Dismissed in Magistrate's Court.

7/28/1927

Material Witness. He is held as a witness in connection to an investigation on associate John Manfrede, who was arrested earlier in the year. Luciano is again discharged.

8/3/1927

Violation National Prohibition Act. United States District Court discharges him.

11/17/1928

Robbery and Assault. George Uffner and Thomas "Fatty" Walsh are arrested with Luciano at his apartment in the Bronx, in connection to the murder of Arnold Rothstein. All of the suspects denied any knowledge of the murder. Police have no evidence to hold them, but the trio is then charged for an October 5th incident. All three are released on November 23rd in Magistrate's Court.

10/29/1929

Grand Larceny. Luciano was wanted, along with Eddie Diamond, for car theft. After Lucky's wounds were tended to (following the *taken for a ride* incident), he was taken into custody. Magistrate's court discharged him.

3/7/1930

Operating a gambling device. Ten deputy sheriffs conduct a raid within a resort hotel in Miami. Upon entering the top floor of the hotel, they discover tables filled with gamblers and cash. A total of $73,575.05 was collected. Sheriffs took $60,090 from one gambler and a pittance of twelve cents from another. Deputies identified two of the gamblers as Joe "The Boss" Masseria and Charles Lucania. Lucky was allegedly the 'banker' and the only person armed. He had a revolver. All were charged with vagrancy and gambling. Lucky was fined $1000 and released.

2/4/1931

Assault first degree. Judge dismisses two indictments against Luciano.

7/4/1931

Investigation. Luciano is arrested in Cleveland Ohio, but released the same day with no charges.

4/21/1932

Disorderly Conduct. Luciano and Meyer Lansky arrive in Chicago on April 18th to meet with Al Capone's *Outfit* members. Police spot the New York gangsters arriving by train and keep tabs on them. They are arrested with Chicago gangsters Paul "The Waiter" Ricca, Sylvester Agoglia, John Senna and Harry Brown. All are discharged in Municipal Court.

7/11/1932

Violation Corporation Ordinance. Another traffic ticket. Luciano is fined $5.

5/23/1933

** Police had both Louis "Lepke" Buchalter and Lucky Luciano in mind following a shootout on Broadway. The incident never made Luciano's rap sheet because no evidence was ever brought forth against him and no arrest was made. Police were merely suspicious because the machine gun fight was waged against Waxey Gorden's allies – a group Dutch Schultz, Luciano and Lepke friends were trying to push out.

10/24/1935

** Investigators in the murder of Arthur "Dutch Schultz" Flegenheimer suspect Charles "Lucky" Luciano and Johnny "The Fox" Torrio were somehow involved. There was no solid evidence to arrest them, and the pair was in Florida at the time.

12/28/1935

Criminal Registration. Luciano arrives in Miami, promptly registering at the police station, as required by law.

4/2/1936

Violation Section 2460, Penal Law. Compulsory Prostitution. Luciano is jailed in Hot Springs Arkansas, but prepared to fight extradition to New York. He has lawyers and bribes working overtime. However, his plans are dashed as detectives take him into custody and return him to New York, on four indictments. Thomas E. Dewey, Special Prosecutor, successfully brings Luciano to court, where on June 7, 1936 he and eight co-defendants are found guilty; Lucky guilty of sixty-two counts. He is sentenced on June 18th to thirty to fifty years. He is immediately taken to Sing Sing Prison, and then on July 2nd, transferred to Clinton Prison – unaffectionately known as *Little Siberia.*

2/22/1947
Undesirable Alien. Luciano is arrested at a café, after leaving his home in the exclusive section of Mirimar Cuba. Secret police question him at the station, then in the immigration office; he admits gangland pals Bugsy Siegel, Meyer Lansky and Frank Costello have visited him. He is not charged with a crime, but on the 27th, he is officially declared "Undesirable" and scheduled for deportation.

** He is arrested in Genoa Italy immediately after arrival from Cuba on April 12. Held for nine days and taken to Palermo.

** Again arrested (June 25), in connection with a cocaine bust, but released and permitted to move to Naples.

** **Admonition.** By the early 1950's, authorities in Naples impose curfew, and revoke his passport and driver's license. He is given back some freedom in 1956, thanks to unconstitutionality ruling of the admonition imposed upon him.

1/26/1962
Suspicion. Luciano is questioned by authorities concerning a Sicily/Spain/United States narcotics smuggling ring.

ACKNOWLEDGEMENTS

To my family, friends and avid readers of true crime mysteries…
I thank you!

Jennifer, Natasha, Kylie, Anthony, Alex, Mom, Ingrid, Jean,
Vince, Debbie, Gary and all my extended family. Gus, Finster,
Mango, Lil Dirt, Tiny, Nutz. And… Dad.

Gerald Posner, Arthur Nash, Pete Forcelli, Thomas Hunt,
Jeffrey Lahurd and the Sarasota County History Center, Ronald
Fino, Seth Ferranti, David Brooks, John Grenke, and the Uffner
Family Source.

Ron Chepesiuk and Dimas Harya.

Illustrations by Natasha Cipollini. Photo Collections by C.
Cipollini and C. Jones.

A.A.P.-Reuter. "Slums Mourning Lucky Luciano." *The Sydney Morning Herald*, January 29, 1962: 1.

Anderson, Jack. "The Last Days of Lucky Luciano." *Parade*, June 17, 1962: 6-7.

AP. "Court Links Erickson With Miami Gambling." June 10, 1950: 18.

—. "Girl Undergoes 16 Hour Grilling." *Fitchburg Sentinel*, 1936 14-July: 6.

—. "Two Waive Extradition." *Lawrence Journal-World*, 1936 15-July.

—. "New York Gangster Bruised and Stabbed Survives The Ride." *Meriden Record*, October 18, 1929: 21.

—. "Gangland Pal Dead in Crash." *Ocala Star Banner*, October 1, 1959: 18.

—. "Man Accused by Schlultz Caught in South." *Pittsburgh Post-Gazette*, 1936 2-April.

—. "Bullets in Back Kill Gang King." *San Antonio Express*, 1931 16-April: 12.

—. "Gift From Russia." *Spokane Daily Chronicle*, 1932 7-January: 6.

—. "Dewey Commutes Luciano Sentence." *Syracuse Post Standard*, January 4, 1946: 5.

—. "Schultz Name The Boss As His Assassin." *The Meridan Daily Journal*, 1935 26-October: 28.

—. "Police Quiz Lansky on Anastasia." *The Miami News*, February 12, 1958: 2A.

—. "Dope Ring Leaders Will Be Indicted By Federal Grand Jury." *The Palm Beach Post*, 1929 11-March: 1.

—. "Five Bandits Rob Manager in Big Theatre." *The Reading Eagle*, 1926 4-January: 1.

Associated Press. "Believe Torrio Was Fixer." *Panama City Herald*, 1935 28-October: 1.

Brooks, David, interview by Cipollini. *The American Gangsters* (September 20, 2013).

Burton Turkus, Sid Feder. *Murder, Inc.: The Story Of The Syndicate*. Da Capo Press, 2003.

Carbondale Free Press. "Cast Doubt On Girl's Story of Branding." 1936 14-July: 1.

Cortes, Josephine. "He Once Helped Save Luciano's Life." *Sarasota Herald-Tribune*, 1962 6-February: 4.

Coshocton Tribune. "Rothstein Shadow Darkens New Murder." 1929 12-March: 2.

FBI. *Memorandum*. Interview, California: FBI, 2004.

Ferranti, Seth, interview by Cipollini. *Author: Rayful Edmond: Washington D.C.'s Most Notorious Drug Lord* (October 27, 2013).

Fino, Ronald, interview by Cipollini. *Former FBI Operative* (October 1, 2013).

Forcelli, Pete, interview by Cipollini. *Special Agent ATF* (September 6, 2013).

Fralfy, Oscar. "Lucky Luciano Though Nickname Misnomer." *Star News*, 1962 19-February: 8.

Gilmore, Eddie. "Claims Killer Mutilated Her." *Mason City Globe Gazette*, 1936 13-July: 2.

Harrison, Paul. "Broadway Night Clubs, Under Police Fire, Are Called Headquarters of Big Gangs." *The Mantiwoc Herald-News*, 1931 2-February: 8.

—. "Chorus Girls Pick Names Out of Sky." *The Milwaukee Journal*, 1934 9-March: 27.

Hunt, Thomas. "Year by Year: Charlie Lucky's Life." *Informer Journal*, 2012 April.

Hunt, Thomas, interview by Cipollini. *Publisher: Informer Journal* (September 30, 2013).

INS. "Luciano Keeps Beauty From Testifying." *Rochester Journal*, 1936 3-June: 3.

—. "Vice Leaders Parade to Testify." *The Arcadia Tribune*, May 26, 1936: 1.

—. "Dope Smuggler is Key Witness." *The Hammond Times*, 1939 2-April: 3.

—. "Two Women Shot During Gang Gunfight." *The San Antonio Light*, 1933 25-May: 3A.

—. "Predict Gang to War Over Murder." *The Van Wert Daily Bulletin*, 1931 16-April: 1.

—. "Rothstein's One Time Bodyguard Arrested." *Wichita Daily Times*, 1928 18-November: 1.

Johnson, Erskine. "Luciano Offers Half A Million to Launder Life Story On Film." *Naugatuck News*, 1952 12-November: 10.

Johnson, Irmis. "Easy Annulments." *The Milwaukee Sentinel*, 1948 8-August: 13.

Lait, Jack. "Broadway and Elsewhere: Opium, Politics, Love." *St. Joseph Gazette*, 1949 2-September: 4.

—. "Broadway and Elsewhere." *The Milwaukee Sentinel*, 1952 14-December: 16.

Lyons, Leonard. "The Lyons Den." *The Independent*, November 6, 1952: 8.

—. "No Report Needed by Ex-First Lady." *The Sumter Daily Item*, April 9, 1966: 1-2.

Mappen, Marc. *Prohibition Gangsters: The Rise & Fall of a Bad Generation.* Rutgers University Press, 2013.

Miami News Wire Service. "Catering to the Beast in Man Made King of Lucky." *The Miami News*, January 28, 1962: 14A.

Miller, Llewellyn. "I Talked With Luciano." *The American Weekly*, 1952 14-December: 5,6,22.

New York Times. "Gang Kills Gunman; 2 Bystanders Hit." 1922 12-August.

New York Times. "Lucania is Called Shallow Parasite." 1936 19-June: 22.

New York Times. "Narcotics King Accuses Torrio." 1939 23-April.

New York Times. "9 Public Enemies Are Freed By Court." *New York Times*, December 25, 1931: 1.

—. "Fight To Upset Law on Gang Round-Ups." *New York Times*, December 16, 1931: 1.

—. "Mulrooney Swears To Evil Repute Of Three." *New York Times*, December 20, 1931: 1.

Newark, Tim. *Boardwalk Gangster: The Real Lucky Luciano.* St. Martins Griffin, 2011.

—. *Mafia Allies: The True Story of America's Secret Alliance with the Mob in World War II.* Zenith Press, 2007.

Pearson, Drew. "Lucky Luciano Talked Frankly to U.S. Agents." *The Tuscaloosa News*, 1962 15-March: 4.

Porter, Darwin. *J. Edgar Hoover and Clyde Tolson: Investigating the Sexual Secrets of America's Most Famous Men and Women* . Blood Moon Productions, 2012.

Poulsen, Ellen. *The Case Against Lucky Luciano: New York's Most Sensational Vice Trial* . Clinton Cook Publishing Corp., 2007.

Reuters. "Luciano Role Gets Threats." *Saskatoon Star-Phoenix*, February 26, 1962.

—. "Luciano Role Gets Threats." *Saskatoon Star-Phoenix*, February 26, 1962: 11.

Ross, George. "New York Column." *The Escinap Daily Press*, 1938 4-June: 4.

—. "Broadway." *The Pittsburgh Press*, 1941 16-November.

—. "Names." *The Vancouver Sun*, 1936 13-October: 6.

Ruark, Robert. "Sinatra Sets Poor Example For Followers." *The Evening Independent*, 1947 22-February: 14.

San Antonio Light. "Arabian Nights Adventures of the Poor Theater Usher." 1937 13-June: 3.

Sell, Robert. "Another Lucky Escape for Unlucky Lucky's Girl." *Albuquerque Journal*, 1939 24-December: 15.

Sid Federer, Joachim Joesten. *The Luciano Story*. Da Capo Press, 1994.

Sifakis, Carl. *The Encyclopedia of American Crime*. New York: Smithmark, 1992.

Soanes, Wood. "Lucky Luciano Dickering For Movie Story of His Life." *Oakland Tribune*, 1952 21-October: 29.

Source, Uffner Family, interview by Cipollini. *Source* (October 21, 2013).

Tamm, Quinn John. *Memorandum for the Record*. FBI Memorandum, Santa Ana: FBI, 2004.

The Bridgeport Telegram. "New Haven Girl Wounded in Bootleggers Fued." 1922 12-August: 1.

The Daily Mail. "Girl Acquitted in Theft Case." 1936 29-August: 3.

The Daily News. "Police Establish Identity of Man Who Branded Girl." 1936 13-July: 1.

The Evening Independent. "Frank Erickson, Alleged Vagrant, Shows Thousands." 1939 14-June.

The Hammond Times. "Johnny Torrio; Lucky Luciano Doze in Miami." 1935 31-October: 1.

The Kingsport Times. "Good Work on Narcotics." 1938 15-December: 4.

The Lowell Sun. "Taken to Baltimore." 1936 19-August: 5.

The Milwaukee Sentinel. "Eight Gang Victim Found Slain With Axe." 1935 6-November: 8.

The Morning Herald. "Lucky's Dear Friend." 1936 24-April: 1.

The Reading Eagle. "Police Hold Gordon Aide." 1933 1-September.

The Salt Lake Tribune. "T'was Showgirls Across the Sea in a New Dizzy Diplomacy." 1935 31-March: 2.

The Tyrone Daily Herald. "Man Taken For a Ride But Lives to Tell About It." 1929 2-December: 7.

Times Daily. "Uncle Sam Spurns Her." 1937 21-August: 1.

Towne, Vincent. "Swiss Intelligence Too Shrewd for Nina." *Pittsburgh Post-Gazette*, 1942 25-August: 20.

UP. "Money to be Made." *Moorehead Daily News*, 1932 21-October: 5.

—. "Woman Calls N.Y. Suspect Vice Ring Head." *Oakland Tribune*, May 22, 1936.

—. "Druggist in Chicago Tortured." *Oelwein Daily Register*, 1929 3-June.

—. "Gamblers Held in Miami Beach Raid." *The Charleston Daily Mail*, 1930 1-March: 1.

—. "Luciano Offers To Star In Movie." *The Pittsburgh Press*, September 28, 1953.

—. "Suspect is Held in Girl Carving." *The Pittsburgh Press*, 1936 15-July: 8.

—. "Mutilated Girl Admits Gangster Story is Hoax." *The Wisconsin State Journal*, 1936 17-July: 5.

UPI. "Former Agent Still Hounding Lucky Luciano." *News-Herald*, February 8, 1973: 2c.

Warner, Richard N. "The Last Word on the Last Testament." *Informer Journal*, 2012 April.

Wilson, Earl. "Lucky Luciano's Homesick, Resents Exile From Havana." *Miami Daily News*, August 22, 1949: 32.

—. "The Midnight Earl." *The Winona Republican-Herald*, 1953 24-September: 4.

Winchell, Walter. "On Broadway." *St. Petersburg Times*, 1948 24-February: 32.

——. "On Broadway." *St. Petersburg Times*, September 25, 1940: 18.